Introduction		2

Section 1	**Understanding English language learners**	5
	English language learners (ELLs) in Ontario schools	5
	Canadian-born English language learners	5
	Newcomers from other countries	6
	Understanding what English language learners bring to Ontario classrooms	7
	Understanding the bilingual advantage	8
	Successful outcomes for English language learners	10
	Learning the language of school	11
	Everyday English proficiency and academic English proficiency	12
	Understanding successful language acquisition	14

Section 2	**Working together to support English language learners**	17
	Building a whole-school approach	18
	Roles and responsibilities in supporting English language	18
	Equity and inclusion in programs for English language learners	22
	Character development	23
	Student success	24
	Planning the registration process	25
	Reception and orientation	25
	Initial assessment	32
	The initial interview	33
	Placement and programming	37
	ESL and ELD programs and delivery models	37
	Monitoring and reporting to parents	40
	Participation of ELLs in large-scale assessments	41
	Classroom assessment and English language learners	42
	Discontinuation of ESL or ELD support	42
	ELLs with Special Education needs	43
	Transition from the elementary to the secondary school program	46

Section 3	**Adapting the Ontario curriculum for English language learners**	49
	Differentiating instruction for English language learners	49
	Program adaptations: Modifications and accommodations	50
	Describing language behaviours – What students can do and are learning to do	51
	Making language and content accessible for English language learners	55
	Strategies to support beginning English language learners	57
	On-going strategies for supporting English language learners	59
	Assessment	61
	Sample adapted unit frameworks	64
	Unit planning Template	65
	Sample adapted unit framework for Grade 2: Movement – Simple machines	66
	Sample adapted unit framework for Grade 5: Early Civilizations – A museum of innovations	74
	Sample adapted unit framework for Grade 7: Interactions in the environment – Responding to an environmental issue	83

Glossary		92
Resources		94
Ontario Ministry of Education resources		96
Appendix: Descriptions of Skills at the Four Stages of Second-Language Acquisition and Literacy Development		99

Introduction

This document replaces *The Ontario Curriculum, Grades 1 – 8: English As a Second Language and English Literacy Development– A Resource Guide, 2001.*

Each school day, two million students attend Ontario's publicly funded schools. They gather together to learn, with one another and from one another; to acquire the skills needed to succeed in school and in life; and to become confident, well-rounded, critical thinkers.

Reach Every Student – Energizing Ontario Education, Ontario Ministry of Education, 2008, p. 2

Ontario schools serve a student population from a rich array of cultural and linguistic backgrounds. Throughout the province, many students in English-language schools are English language learners (ELLs) – students who are learning the language of instruction at the same time as they are learning the curriculum and developing a full range of literacy skills.

More teachers than ever before are responding to the specific kinds of challenges that these students bring with them to the classroom. Teachers are also learning that the results can be inspiring, exciting, and rewarding for everyone.

All students, including English language learners, are expected to meet the rigorous challenges of the Ontario curriculum. Effective language and literacy instruction begins with the needs of the learner clearly in mind, and all teachers – across all content areas – are teachers of both language and literacy. Their success is a shared responsibility. Teachers and administrators are working together with parents to ensure that all of Ontario's students are ready to take their place in a cohesive and productive society.

Literacy is defined as "the ability to use language and images in rich and varied forms to read, write, listen, view, represent, and think critically about ideas. It involves the capacity to access, manage, and evaluate information; to think imaginatively and analytically, and to communicate thoughts and ideas effectively. Literacy includes critical thinking and reasoning to solve problems and make decisions related to issues of fairness, equity, and social justice. Literacy connects individuals and communities, and is an essential tool for personal growth and active participation in a cohesive, democratic society."

Reach Every Student – Energizing Ontario Education. Ontario Ministry of Education, 2008, p. 2

This resource is one in a series written to assist classroom teachers in supporting a growing demographic within Ontario schools – English language learners. The goal is to help teachers understand the kinds of supports that English language learners require to learn the English and content of the classroom. The focus is on making learning visible and accessible for English language learners who face their own unique challenges but, more importantly, who present a rich resource in classrooms throughout the province.

In preparing this resource, the Ministry of Education acknowledges the valuable work being done in schools and classrooms across Ontario, and the dedication of teachers throughout the province in creating an inclusive learning environment that supports the success of every student.

The term *parent* is used throughout this document to refer to the legal guardian of any student under 18 years of age.

Understanding English language learners

English language learners in Ontario schools

English language learners are students in provincially funded English language schools whose first language is a language other than English, or is a variety of English that is significantly different from the variety used for instruction in Ontario's schools, and who may require focussed educational supports to assist them in attaining proficiency in English.

These students may be Canadian born or recently arrived from other countries. They come from diverse backgrounds and school experiences, and have a wide variety of strengths and needs.

English is an international language, and many varieties of English – sometimes referred to as dialects – are spoken around the world. Standard English is the variety of English that is used as the language of education, law, and government in English-speaking countries. Some varieties of English are very different – not only in pronunciation or accent but also in vocabulary and sentence structure – from the English required for success in Ontario schools. Some varieties are so different from standard English that many linguists consider them to be languages in their own right.

English Language Learners/ESL and ELD Programs and Services: Policies and Procedures for Ontario Elementary and Secondary Schools, Kindergarten to Grade 12, 2007, 1.2.

The term English language learner (ELL) has come into increasing use internationally among educators and researchers because it distinguishes the students themselves from the programs that support their language learning needs.
Many Roots, Many Voices, 2005

L1 is the term that may be used in place of *first language* or *home language*.

Canadian-born English language learners

Many English language learners were born in Canada and raised in families or communities in which languages other than English are spoken. They may include, for example:

- Aboriginal students whose first language is a language other than English;
- children who were born in communities that have maintained a distinct cultural and linguistic tradition, who have a first language that is not English, and who attend English language schools; and
- children who were born in immigrant communities in which languages other than English are primarily spoken.

The Ministry of Education is dedicated to excellence in public education for all students, including First Nation, Métis, and Inuit students. The document *Ontario First Nation, Métis, and Inuit Education Policy Framework, 2007* provides the strategic policy context within which the Ministry of Education, school boards, and schools will work together to improve the academic achievement of First Nation, Métis, and Inuit students. The framework has two components: targeted strategies and supports for First Nation, Métis, and Inuit students; and strategies to increase knowledge and awareness of Aboriginal histories, cultures, and perspectives among all students, teachers, and school board staff. In order to achieve these goals, a holistic approach integrating the framework strategies throughout all programs, services, and initiatives is necessary.

Section 23 of the Canadian Charter of Rights and Freedoms defines the right of Canadian citizens of the English-speaking or French-speaking minority of a province to educate their children in that minority language, wherever numbers warrant. In Ontario, francophone children who come within the defined classes, and who are otherwise qualified to be resident pupils, have the right to be educated in French language schools at both the elementary and secondary levels.

English Language Learners/ESL and ELD Programs and Services: Policies and Procedures for Ontario Elementary and Secondary Schools, Kindergarten to Grade 12, 2007, 1.2.

Newcomers from other countries

Newcomers arrive from countries around the world at various stages in their educational careers. They may arrive in their pre-school years or at any point between Kindergarten and Grade 12. They may arrive at the beginning of the school year or at any time during the school year. Depending on their age and country of origin, they may have had varying educational experiences prior to their arrival in Canada, and consequently will require different levels of support in order to succeed in the classroom.

Newcomers from other countries may include:

- children who have arrived in Canada with their families as part of a voluntary, planned immigration process. If they are of school age, they have most often received formal education in their home countries, and some may have studied English as a foreign language. However, some of these students may have had limited or inconsistent access to schooling.

- children who have arrived in Canada as a result of a war or other crisis in their home country, and who may have left their homeland under conditions of extreme urgency. These children have often suffered traumatic experiences, and may also be separated from family members. They may have been in transit for a number of years, or may not have had access to formal education in their home country or while in transit.

- international, or visa, students who have paid fees to attend school in Ontario and often plan to attend a Canadian university. Most visa students are of secondary school age. These students typically arrive in Canada without their families, and may live with extended family, a host family, or alone. Because they often represent the aspirations of their families, and because of the expense involved in sending them to study in Canada, these students are often under great pressure to do well and progress through school as quickly as possible. Some have had instruction in English but may still have considerable difficulty learning English in Ontario classrooms.

Children of parents who do not meet Section 23 criteria can be admitted to Ontario's French language schools by an admissions committee. Though they may be from any background, they are often the children of parents who have settled in Canada as immigrants or refugees, and for whom French is their first, second, or even third language, yet who feel a certain attachment to French. They often come from countries where the language of public administration or schooling is French.

English Language Learners/ESL and ELD Programs and Services: Policies and Procedures for Ontario Elementary and Secondary Schools, Kindergarten to Grade 12, 2007, 1.2.

Understanding what English language learners bring to Ontario classrooms

English language learners are a richly heterogeneous group. The paths they take to acquire a new language and to adjust to their new environment are also varied and in keeping with their unique needs and experiences.

English language learners bring to Ontario schools a wide variety of life situations and understandings and a range of educational experiences. Within the safe and welcoming classroom environment, teachers are given a unique opportunity to tap the rich resource of knowledge and understandings that ELLs bring to school, and which, in turn, enrich the learning of all students in the classroom. The role of the school and the teacher is critical in supporting their identities and development as bilingual learners, and in helping ELLs shape a vision of the future in which they will take their place as Canadian citizens in a global economy.

This country is your country. It's up to you to give it your imagination, your talent, your view of the world. And you know what? I believe that nothing is impossible for children like you... who have courage, heart and a head brimming with ideas.

Michaëlle Jean, Governor-General of Canada

Understanding the bilingual advantage

Students who see their previously developed language skills acknowledged by their teachers and parents are more likely to feel confident and take the risks involved in learning a new language. They are able to view English as an *addition* to their first language, rather than as a *substitution* for it.

There are numerous positive outcomes that result from continuing to promote the ongoing use and development of ELLs' first languages. Respect and use of the first language contribute both to the building of a confident learner and to the efficient learning of additional languages and academic achievement, including:

- developing mental flexibility;
- developing problem-solving skills;
- communicating with family members;
- experiencing a sense of cultural stability and continuity;
- understanding cultural and family values;
- developing awareness of global issues;
- expanding career opportunities.

Students who are able to communicate and are literate in more than one language are better prepared to participate in a global society. Though this has benefits for the individual, Canadian society also stands to gain from having a multilingual workforce. The children now entering Ontario schools are a valuable resource for Canada.

Experts tell us

... does the school language policy view students as bilingual, with talents in both their home language and English, or just as learners of English whose home language is irrelevant to academic success?

> Jim Cummins, *Promoting Literacy in Multilingual Contexts, Research Monograph #5,*
> The Literacy and Numeracy Secretariat, Ontario Ministry of Education, 2007. p. 3

Students with well-developed skills in their first language have been shown to acquire an additional language more easily and fully and that, in turn, has a positive impact on academic achievement.

> Fred Genesee, Kathryn Lindholm-Leary, William Saunders, and Donna Christian. Educating English
> Language Learners: A Synthesis of Research Evidence. Cambridge University Press, 2006.

ELLs use what they know in one language to help develop other languages. This positive transfer effect has been found to be particularly strong in reading.

> Claude Goldenberg. "Teaching English Language Learners: What the Research
> Does – and Does Not – Say," *American Educator,* Summer 2008: 8-23.

English language learners are extremely resourceful learners with a unique bilingual reservoir of skills and experiences.

> *Fred Genesee, from a speech at TESOL 2008, "Learning to read a second language:*
> *What does the research say and what do we do about it?"*

The development of two languages in childhood turns out to be a profound event that ripples through the life of that individual.

> Ellen Bialystok, *Bilingualism in Development.* Cambridge University Press, 2001, 247-248.

Students who use their bilingual skills have been shown to develop both cognitive flexibility and divergent thinking.

> Jim Cummins, "The Influence of Bilingualism on Cognitive Growth: A Synthesis of Research
> Findings and Explanatory Hypotheses" in Colin Baker and Nancy H. Hornberger, eds.,
> *An Introductory Reader to the Writings of Jim Cummins.* Multilingual Matters, 2001.

Successful outcomes for English language learners

Experts tell us

Although the acquisition of second-language skills is important for young learners ... second language acquisition is not the most important task they face. Their academic achievement and social integration are far more important. Second-language learning, therefore, needs to be recast as a means to greater ends.

Jean Handscombe, "Putting It All Together" *In Fred Genesee, ed., Educating Second Language Children: The Whole Child, the Whole Curriculum, the Whole Community.* Cambridge: Cambridge University Press, 1994.

ELLs in Grades 1 - 8 receive ESL or ELD programs and services to help them achieve success as they learn the language and content of their grade's curriculum.

A vision for the successful English language learner, developed by educators from across the province is included in *The Ontario Curriculum Grades 9 - 12 English as a Second Language and English Literacy Development,* 2007.

Successful English language learners can:

- use English to communicate effectively in a variety of social settings;
- use English to achieve academically in all content areas;
- take charge of their own learning, independently and in groups;
- use effective learning strategies;
- integrate confidently into classrooms or courses;
- use English effectively to advocate for themselves;
- be successful in their chosen post-secondary destination;
- function effectively in an information and technology-based society;
- use critical-literacy and critical-thinking skills to interpret the world around them;
- participate in the social, economic, political, and cultural life of their own communities and of Canada.

ELLs may be unable to demonstrate their true competence in subject content areas due to their current English language skills. The role of the school is to assist these students in acquiring both the English skills and content knowledge they need to participate in learning activities equally with their peers and to meet the expectations of the Ontario curriculum.

Learning the language of school

> All English language learners] ... need to learn the language of instruction in English language schools at the same time as they are working towards meeting the curriculum expectations.
>
> *English Language Learners/ESL and ELD Programs and Services: Policies and Procedures for Ontario Elementary and Secondary Schools, Kindergarten to Grade 12,* **2007, 1.1: Introduction.**

Young children learn the sound system of a new language more effectively than older learners. They may acquire a local accent quickly, whereas their older siblings may always have an accent influenced by the sound system of their home language. But young children may well take five or more years to catch up to their age peers in vocabulary acquisition and the accurate use of grammar in both spoken and written English. This is because they also need to develop fundamental concepts and literacy skills that they may not have developed in their home language.

Katharine Davies Samway and Denise McKeon, *Myths and Realities: Best Practices for English Language Learners,* 2nd edition Portsmouth, NH: Heinemann, 2007, p. 28-30.

ELLs are required to understand and negotiate increasingly complex texts, especially in the junior grades and beyond. Colin Baker and Nancy H. Hornberger, eds., *An Introductory Reader to the Writings of Jim Cummins,* Clevedon, UK: Multilingual Matters, 2001.

Older students have more English to learn and less time left in school. However, they have an advantage because most are already literate in their first language, have had more school experience, and have a wider range of prior knowledge. They may acquire vocabulary and grammatical structures in English more efficiently because their first language is more developed.

Some students come with little or no schooling and lack basic literacy skills in any language. Those students are at particular risk of failing to thrive in their new educational environment and will require focussed instruction to develop both concepts and language skills.

D. Watt and H. Roessingh, "The Dynamics of ESL Drop-outs: Plus ça change...". *Canadian Modern Language Review, 58,* 2001: 203-222.

An implication ... is that second-language students will typically require additional support to gain access to the language of the curriculum and to harvest the language of academic texts. Jim Cummins, "The Challenge of Learning Academic Language," *A Guide to Effective Literacy Instruction: Grades 4 to 6, Volume One, Foundations of Literacy Instruction for the Junior Learner,* p. 24

Teachers can sometimes be misled by the high degree of oral proficiency demonstrated by many English language learners in their use of everyday English, and may mistakenly conclude that these ELLs are equally proficient in their Academic English use. ELLs who have developed oral proficiency in everyday English will still require instructional scaffolding to meet curriculum expectations.

Everyday English proficiency and academic English proficiency

In order to participate in the curriculum learning taking place in their classrooms, English language learners must master two distinct forms of English language: Everyday English proficiency and Academic English proficiency.

Experts tell us

Research in second-language acquisition (Wayne & Collier; 2003, Cummins, 2006) indicates that most English language learners can function well in social situations and in visually contextualized classroom activities within a year or two. Most take much longer – five years or more – to catch up to their age peers in using the language to communicate complex academic concepts.

Everyday English proficiency, often referred to as *basic interpersonal communication skills,* is relatively easy for most ELLs to master, usually within a year or two, because the vocabulary and language skills directly relate to their immediate surroundings, daily lives, and needs. Strong Everyday English proficiency enables ELLs to communicate more effectively with their teachers and peers, to integrate into their new school environments, and to interact comfortably with English speakers outside of school.

Academic English proficiency, often referred to *as cognitive academic language proficiency,* is more difficult to acquire and takes much longer, often five or more years. The development of increasingly complex uses of language to express and explore concepts is at the core of education. ELLs are working hard to catch up to a moving target – they are learning the language of instruction at the same time as they are learning the grade curriculum. ELLs must learn to talk, read, and write about abstract concepts. In addition to learning vocabulary and language structures, Academic English proficiency often involves learning new ways of thinking, such as describing properties or processes, comparing and contrasting, hypothesizing, and generalizing. The demands of Academic English proficiency increase as ELLs progress through Grades 1-8 and encounter more abstract material across the range of subject areas within the Ontario curriculum.

Although beginners start by developing oral fluency and Everyday English language proficiency, they need opportunities to develop Academic English language proficiency in the content areas immediately, such as subject-specific terminology and grammatical constructions that are almost never used in daily conversation.

Key differences between everyday language and academic language	
Everyday language proficiency includes:	Academic language proficiency includes:
the ability to maintain a face-to-face conversation with peers and with a variety of school personnel in various settings, inside and outside the classroom	the ability to understand when there is less opportunity for interaction (e.g., when listening to a presentation or reading a textbook)
the ability to talk, read, or write about familiar content or about what is happening here and now	the ability to talk, read, and write about content that has fewer connections to prior learning or personal experience, is more abstract, and is more distant in space or time (e.g., learning about the water cycle, studying the earth's crust, or learning about Canada's provinces)
knowledge about basic vocabulary/high frequency words such as *old*, *food*, *tired*, *cars*, or *trucks*	knowledge of more sophisticated, low frequency vocabulary such as *ancient*, *nutrition*, *fatigued*, or *vehicles*
the ability to use simple sentences and the active voice such as: *We heated the water until it boiled. We used a thermometer to measure the temperature.*	the ability to use more complex sentences and grammatical structures such as: *When the water was heated to the boiling point, a thermometer was used to measure the temperature.*

Experts tell us

Students who see their previously developed language skills acknowledged by their teachers and parents are also more likely to feel confident and to take the risks involved in learning in their new school environment. They are able to view English as an *addition* to their first language, rather than a *replacement* for it.

Elizabeth Coelho, *Adding English: A Guide to Teaching in Multilingual Classrooms.*
Pippin, 2004, Introduction.

Understanding successful language acquisition

The rate at which an English language learner develops proficiency in English, adapts to the new environment, and integrates into the academic program is influenced by a variety of factors.

General factors

In addition to a well-developed first language, there are a number of other factors that may make children more or less willing and able to engage in the task of learning a new language. Initial assessment of, and ongoing enquiry about, children's background experiences and accomplishments will provide helpful information on items such as:

- *The adjustment process*
  All newcomer families experience a period of cultural adjustment. Individuals adjust to this phase in different ways and at different rates. The adjustment process can be particularly complex for ELLs who have experienced trauma.

- *Prior experience with English*
  Both newcomer and Canadian-born ELLs may have developed English skills before their arrival in Ontario schools. However, some students may be reluctant to display those skills in the school setting.

- *Previous schooling*
  ELLs will vary widely in their initial comfort with the curriculum and culture of the new school environment, based on previous personal experiences in school.

  Some students arrive having had no interruption in their education, while, for a variety of reasons, others have had limited prior schooling. The latter will require ELD support.

- *The presence of learning exceptionalities*
  English language learners are likely to have the same range of learning exceptionalities as other Ontario students, and some of these exceptionalities will influence the ease with which they develop English language skills.

- *Personality factors*
  Some students will seek opportunities in which to use the new language and to take the risks involved in experimenting with English. Others may prefer to wait until they know that they can "get it right."

- *Motivational factors*
  Students will learn a language more easily if they identify with others who regularly use the new language, and if their identity is not threatened by negative social relations or feelings of intimidation within the new setting.

  Kelleen Toohey, *Learning English at School: Identity, Social Relations and Classroom Practice.* Clevedon, UK: Multilingual Matters, 2000.

School and classroom factors

A number of school and classroom factors have a positive influence on English language acquisition. These include:

- *The classroom environment*
  ELLs thrive in a welcoming environment in which teachers and peers:
  - value them as a positive presence in the classroom and the school;
  - encourage their efforts at learning English and sharing their knowledge of the world;
  - encourage their use of their L1;
  - provide books, visual representations, and concrete objects that reflect their backgrounds and interests.

- *The amount and quality of language learning support*
  ELLs benefit when teachers select approaches and strategies that are specifically differentiated in response to the individual student's language learning needs.

- *Opportunities for interaction in English*
  ELLs need frequent opportunities for extended conversation in English with their peers and other members of the larger community. They benefit from regular opportunities to hear English used in situations where they are able to understand at least the basics of what is being said and opportunities to try out their developing skills in low-stakes situations.

  > Merrill Swain, *"The Output Hypothesis: Theory and Research," in Eli Hinkel, ed., Handbook on Research in Second Language Teaching and Learning.* Lawrence Erlbaum, 2005, 471-484.

- *Supportive language feedback*
  "Errors" are a normal part of second-language learning; some errors are the result of ELLs working out the grammatical rules of English in the same way as all speakers do when learning their first language, while others are a result of the influence of the ELL's first language.

  ELLs benefit from opportunities to receive feedback in a respectful and encouraging way. It is helpful when teachers respond first to the content of what the student is saying or writing, before rephrasing, in order to provide a model for the student. Teachers should focus on one or two errors at a time, rather than trying to "fix" everything.

  > Patsy M. Lightbown and Nina Spada. *How Languages Are Learned*, 3rd ed., Oxford University Press, 2006.

- *Involving and Supporting the Parent Community*
  Everyone in the school needs to make parents feel welcomed. Students are more successful when their parents are involved in their education. (Deforges, 2003)

  When schools reach out to the parent community, it is important to recognize that some parents will have had educational experiences that are significantly different from those of Ontario-born parents, or may have limited English proficiency. It is the role of the school to ensure that all parents can access and engage with the school community.

Working together to support English language learners

> School boards will design programs and services for English language learners so that they are flexible in response to changing needs and reflective of the needs of the students.
>
> ***English Language Learners/ESL and ELD Programs and Services: Policies and Procedures for Ontario Elementary and Secondary Schools, Kindergarten to Grade 12, 2007, 2.5.3.***

Every day, more than one million English language learners attend Ontario's publicly funded schools. They come from every country and every circumstance. They bring with them a valuable world perspective needed by all students to operate successfully in a global community. Their parents come with the hopes that their children will achieve what they could not have achieved elsewhere. Through shared responsibility, our schools need to optimize the synergies within themselves, the parent community, and supporting community partners in order to ensure that all English language learners achieve their fullest potential.

The goal of reaching every student, inclusive of personal circumstances, through a commitment to higher achievement and reduced gaps in performance, recognizes that everyone in a school community has an important role to play in supporting English language learners. All teachers work collaboratively to plan student learning and to evaluate and improve their own instructional strategies. Principals ensure teachers and support staff (including office staff) have what they need to be successful. In addition, parents and community partners are welcome in schools and are given opportunities to be active in school life.

Experts tell us

> Shared responsibility incorporates a set of principles and techniques that give members of the school community the authority and responsibility to create what is needed, based on the data and culture of their particular school ...
>
> Collaboration ... is about creating an environment – through structures, systems, processes, and policies – where everyone contributes skills, knowledge, and experience to continuously improve student learning. Collaboration also extends beyond the school's walls ...
>
> Anne Conzemius and Jan O'Neill, *Building Shared Responsibility for Student Learning, Association for Supervision and Curriculum Development*, 2001, p. 2

Building a whole-school approach

Creating a welcoming and inclusive school environment for English language learners is a whole-school responsibility requiring the commitment of administrators, teachers, support staff, and other leaders within the school community. The outcome of this committed effort is a dynamic and vibrant school environment that celebrates linguistic and cultural diversity as an asset, and enriches the learning experience of all students.

Roles and responsibilities in supporting English language learners

The school administrative team

> School boards will designate appropriately qualified personnel to coordinate programs and provide leadership at the system level.
>
> *English Language Learners/ESL and ELD Programs and Services: Policies and Procedures for Ontario Elementary and Secondary Schools, Kindergarten to Grade 12, 2007, 2.5.2.*

The school administrative team works in partnership with all staff, parents, and appropriate community partners to ensure that every student has access to the best possible educational experience. To build the capacity of the whole school in helping English language learners reach their full potential, the school administrative team should:

- ensure that the school has procedures and practices in place for welcoming newly arrived English language learners and their families;
- build an inclusive and welcoming environment for all students and their families through the use of materials in community languages, the provision of interpreters whenever possible, and the recognition of diversity in school events and messages;
- encourage involvement of newcomer parents in school events and the parent council;
- acquire and make available a range of resources in classrooms and in the school library that reflect the linguistic and cultural makeup of the school community;
- ensure that the planning of programs to support ELLs is coordinated by a person with expertise in ESL/ELD;
- support all teachers in incorporating appropriate curriculum adaptations and teaching strategies into their instruction and assessment to meet the needs of English language learners;
- provide access to quality professional development for all school staff;
- facilitate collaboration time to enrich and extend teachers' repertoire of instructional and assessment strategies to meet the needs of English language learners;

- review and discuss with staff the most recent demographic information on the school community;
- create and nurture links with community partners such as school settlement workers and community ethno-cultural organizations where available.

Teachers

Teachers bring knowledge, enthusiasm, and varied teaching and assessment approaches to the classroom, addressing individual student needs and ensuring sound and challenging learning opportunities for every student.

In supporting English language learners, teachers:

- learn about their students' backgrounds, experiences, and languages;
- provide engaging and challenging opportunities for English language development for all learners with appropriate modifications/ accommodations, as needed;
- use a variety of instructional, assessment, and evaluation strategies that are designed to facilitate the success of English language learners;
- collaborate with the person responsible for ELLs to plan for the needs of the English language learners in their classrooms;
- create a classroom environment which reflects and celebrates the linguistic and cultural diversity of all students;
- support English language learners in their integration into the academic and social life of the school;
- communicate effectively with parents, taking into account the varied background experiences of diverse families;
- work together to increase the capacity of the whole school in meeting the needs of English language learners.

Students

Students have many responsibilities with regard to their learning, and these increase as they advance through elementary school. Students benefit when they:

- make a sincere commitment to learning and to the development of co-operative skills in the classroom;
- pursue various opportunities outside the classroom to enrich their learning;
- seek out recreational reading materials and multimedia works in English and their home language to extend their knowledge of the world around them;
- engage in conversation with parents, peers, and teachers about what they are reading, writing, and learning;
- take increasing responsibility for their own progress and learning.

Parents

> Parents will be made aware of the goal of ESL and ELD programs in Ontario Schools and how they are of benefit to students who are developing proficiency in English.
>
> *English Language Learners/ESL and ELD Programs and Services: Policies and Procedures for Ontario Elementary and Secondary Schools, Kindergarten to Grade 12, 2007, 2.2.1a*

It is the school's responsibility to provide opportunities for parents of diverse ethno-cultural backgrounds to become engaged, to recognize parents as partners, and to appreciate that their involvement may take different forms. In serving culturally diverse communities, schools need to keep in mind that parents may have different ideas about how, where, and when they should be involved in their children's schooling.

Parents play a very important role in supporting student learning. Studies consistently show that students perform better in school if their parents are involved in their education. (Deforges, 2003) They need not be proficient in English themselves in order to help and support their children in school. They may face barriers to full involvement in the school partnership model, such as limited time or limited proficiency in English.

To support English language learners, parents are strongly encouraged to:

- read to their children, in the home language and/or English, on a regular basis;
- become familiar with the curriculum and what their children are expected to learn at school;
- involve their children in talking about their school experiences;
- attend parent-teacher interviews;
- speak with their child's teacher or appropriate school personnel whenever they have questions or concerns about the program or their child's progress;
- participate in parent workshops and other community events which help them to learn more about the Ontario school system;
- encourage their children to develop and maintain active use of the home language;
- partner effectively with school staff to help their children achieve their goals.

Communication with the home needs to be handled in an honest, sensitive, and respectful manner. This communication can take many forms, both informal and formal: a phone call, a note, a newsletter, a meeting, an interview, a student's agenda/planner, and the school website. When needed, that communication should be available in the home language of the family.

Parents and their ethno-cultural communities often serve as resources that schools can access to assist English language learners and to enrich the cultural environment for everyone in the school.
Many Roots, Many Voices, 2005

Resources for parents

Schools can order printed copies of the following resources or parents can download the resources in a variety of languages

http://www.edu.gov.on.ca/abc123/

- Make Reading Fun
- 10 Tips to Help Your Child with Reading
- 10 Tips to Help Your Child with Writing
- 10 Tips to Help Your Child with Math
- 10 Tips to Help Your Child with Homework
- 10 Tips to Help Boys with Reading
- 10 Tips to Get Your Child Ready for School
- 10 Tips to Help You Communicate with the Teacher
- 10 Tips that Use Arts and Crafts to Develop Math and Literacy Skills
- Tips for Summer Learning Fun
- Does Your Child Need Extra Help?
- Helping Your Child Do Mathematics – A Guide for Parents Kindergarten to Grade 6
- Helping Your Child With Reading and Writing – A Guide for Parents Kindergarten to Grade 6

Community partners

Community partners can be an important resource in students' English language development and success at school. They can provide support for students' literacy and learning needs, both in the classroom and as living models of how the curriculum relates to life beyond school.

To support English language learners, community partners can be invited to:
- connect new families immediately with a contact person of the same cultural/language background, a settlement worker, or a community service provider;
- share information on community-based homework clubs, or start a school-based homework club;
- collaborate with school boards to offer:
  - community-based literacy programs for youth in schools, public libraries, and community centres

- a variety of other school-based supports, such as breakfast clubs and recreation programs
- workshops based on families' needs and interests (e.g., completing income tax returns, job searches, and interview skills)

- offer information and organize workshops and events for families to provide additional information on all aspects of the Ontario school system, as well as on post-secondary pathways;

- provide links to Citizenship and Immigration Canada and other government and community programs which provide support for newcomers;

- offer a school volunteer training program to build parent confidence and involvement (e.g., sessions providing coaching on being a reading buddy or a library assistant);

- foster mentoring services (e.g., parent mentors for other parents, community mentors for parents, parent mentors for students, or community mentors for students).

Equity and inclusion in programs for English language learners

Insight

Equity and excellence go hand-in-hand ... a quality education for all in publicly funded schools is a key feature of fostering social cohesion – an inclusive society where diversity is the hallmark, and where all cultures are embraced within a common set of values.

Reach Every Student – Energizing Ontario Education. Ontario Ministry of Education, 2008, p. 8

The implementation of equity and inclusionary practices in education influences all aspects of school life. It promotes a school climate that encourages all students to work to high standards, affirms the worth of all students, and helps them strengthen their sense of identity and develop a positive self-image. It encourages staff and students to value and show respect for diversity in the school and society at large. It requires schools to adopt measures to provide a safe environment for learning, free from harassment, bullying, violence, and expressions of hate. It encourages students to think critically about themselves and others in the world around them in order to promote fairness, healthy relationships, and active, responsible citizenship.

Opportunities to support the principles of equity and inclusion specific to ELLs include:

- enabling ELLs to develop a sense of personal identity and belonging by sharing information about their own languages and cultures, as well as their experiences in their countries of origin and as newcomers to Canada;
- developing ELLs' understanding of themselves as fully participating citizens in a dynamically changing and evolving Canadian identity of which they are integral parts;
- teaching them directly about their rights and responsibilities as students and citizens;
- reinforcing students' self-identity by providing inclusive learning resources and materials representative of diverse cultures, backgrounds, and experiences;
- including dual language and multilingual resources in the school library and in classroom resources;
- choosing resources on the basis of their appeal for both girls and boys and suited to different levels of English language proficiency;
- respecting aspects of intercultural communication (e.g., awareness that refraining from making eye contact is a sign of respect for persons in positions of authority);
- using global events as opportunities for instruction and being aware of how they may affect students;
- teaching inclusive, non-discriminatory language (e.g., *letter carrier* instead of *mailman*).

Character development

Insight

Academic achievement within a culture of high expectations for learning for all students, from all backgrounds and circumstances, remains the primary responsibility of schools. A number of research findings indicate that character development and the creation of caring and engaging school cultures have the potential to improve student achievement. Excellence in education includes character development.

Finding Common Ground: Character Development in Ontario Schools, K-12. Ontario Ministry of Education, June 2008, p. 18-19

Character development is the deliberate effort to nurture the character attributes upon which schools and communities find consensus. The principles and attributes of character development are universal. They transcend physical and intellectual ability; gender, racial, ethno-cultural, linguistic, and religious differences; and other demographic factors.

At its best, character development supports the whole student – the cognitive, affective, and behavioural domains – facilitating the individual's development both as a learner and as an engaged citizen. Character development contributes to respectful, caring, safe, and inclusive school environments that are pre-requisites for learning. It creates learning communities that are collaborative in which teachers spend less time disciplining and more time doing what they do best – teaching.

Character development must be a whole-school effort, with the expectation that all members of the staff will be committed to its effective implementation and will model, teach, and expect demonstrations of the universal character attributes in all school, classroom, and extracurricular activities.

When newcomer ELLs first enter Ontario schools, principles of character development – as demonstrated in the welcoming learning environment of the receiving school — shape the initial impression that these students form of their new school community. The safe and nurturing school, as exemplified by these principles, serves to provide a setting in which newcomer students learn, grow, and thrive.

Student success

We want our students to learn to think critically, feel deeply, and act wisely.
Finding Common Ground: Character Development in Ontario Schools, K-12. Ontario Ministry of Education, June 2008, p. 17

Every school with Grades 7 and 8 has a Student Success Team that includes, at a minimum, a Student Success Teacher, the principal or designate, a Guidance counsellor (when available), and Special Education teachers. This team should include a member with expertise in teaching ELLs who collaborates with classroom teachers when an English language learner is being supported by the Student Success Team. It meets regularly to ensure the effective delivery of all student success initiatives and to track, coordinate, and assume responsibility for at-risk students including ELLs who are at risk.

The Grades 7-12 Student Success Strategy has five key goals:
- a good outcome for every student
- connecting with students by providing new and relevant learning opportunities
- building on students' interests and strengths
- effective transitions from elementary to secondary school and from secondary to postsecondary
- increasing graduation and reducing drop-out rates

There is a wealth of information, support, and resources about the Student Success initiative available at *http://www.edu.gov.on.ca/studentsuccess*

During the transition from Grade 8 to Grade 9, it may be determined that an English language learner is at risk of disengaging from secondary school.

The Student Success Teacher and Student Success Team can

- provide opportunities for ELLs to visit the secondary school and meet teachers and students before the first day;
- facilitate communication between the elementary and secondary teachers to share known helpful strategies that assist with the learning;
- provide incoming ELLs with a first semester timetable that matches strengths and interests;
- designate a caring adult to the ELL;
- develop early monitoring and intervention strategies that support courses and classroom experiences;
- ensure ELLs are aware of the range of learning and programming opportunities available to them both within the school and across the system.

Planning the registration process

School boards will develop protocols to define procedures and practices for welcoming English language learners and their families and providing them with appropriate orientation to the Ontario school system, in the first language of the students and their families whenever possible. The protocol will include procedures for the admission of students in all grades, including Kindergarten – regardless of level of English proficiency or prior schooling – who arrive and need to begin school in Ontario at any time during the school year.

English Language Learners ESL /ELD Programs and Services: Policies and Procedures for Ontario Elementary and Secondary Schools, Kindergarten to Grade 12, 2007, 2.2.1.

The registration process includes four major components:
- Reception and orientation
- Initial assessment
- Placement and program
- Monitoring and reporting

Since these protocols will reflect the specific demographics of each area, they may look quite different across and within boards.

Reception and orientation

Supportive reception and orientation of new students and their families is a critical first step in the successful integration of English language learners into elementary schools. First impressions are important, and everyone in the school needs to make all parents feel welcome.

A *welcoming* school is an inviting place for students, staff, parents, and visitors. Staff members make concerted efforts to help other members of the school community feel connected and included.

For a complete list of documents needed for school registration available in 18 languages, see Getting Ready for School *at* www.settlement.org

What a welcoming school looks like

- All staff is aware of and understands the process for receiving English language learners and their families.
- There is a school reception team (e.g., administrator, office administrative assistant, ESL/ELD teacher, interpreter, and settlement worker, where available).
- Families are informed about the necessary documentation for school registration.
- There is a designated, comfortable place for the family and reception team to meet and share information.
- Ample time is dedicated for the intake interview and for orientation information about school and basic routines.
- There is access to competent adult interpreters who can assist parents and help them fill out forms.
- There is a program for specially trained student helpers, such as student ambassadors, to orient the new students to the school. They can assist in a variety of important ways:
    - conducting a guided tour of the school;
    - explaining the ways that parents can contact the school in the event of absence, late arrival, or early leaving;
    - outlining safety procedures (e.g., what to do in a fire drill);
    - showing the procedures for borrowing books or using school equipment and technology;
    - providing details to facilitate and encourage entry into sports programs, clubs, and other extracurricular activities;
    - making introductions to students with similar interests;
    - explaining lunchtime procedures.
- Multilingual signs, in the languages of the community, are visible in the school.
- There are efforts to build cross-cultural understandings.
- Information is available in a variety of languages about community resources (e.g., libraries, community centres, adult ESL classes, places of worship, cultural organizations).
- Parents are regularly invited into the classrooms and the school to celebrate student work.
- Space is provided for families to gather if possible (e.g., a room to sit, drink coffee or tea, and read announcements in home languages or meet fellow parents).

Guides explaining the Ontario education system are available for newcomer families to download in various languages. Videos are also available on topics that are important to newcomer parents and students. For more information, visit *www.settlement.org*

Also available on this site:
- The Newcomers' Guide to Elementary Schools
- Parent Teacher Interviews
- Your Library

Insight

Schools can be surprisingly intimidating places for many parents. Newcomers to Canada, in particular, may have experienced a very different school setting, and may therefore be unfamiliar with the school environment. The Ministry of Education offers tips for creating a school climate that makes parents feel comfortable and welcome: *http://www.edu.gov.on.ca/eng/parents/involvement/welcomemat.html*

What diversity in a school looks like

- Bulletin-board displays reflect the cultural backgrounds of the students in the school, and photographic displays depict students of various ethno-cultural backgrounds engaged in a variety of school activities.
- Educational displays represent individuals from many cultures (e.g., well-known personalities, famous inventors, or historical figures).
- Staff members greet parents as they drop off or pick up their children, using a few greetings from different languages.
- Announcements of school meetings and events are made in the home languages of the community.
- Meetings are held with groups of parents to focus on their concerns or on topics of specific interest.
- Special evenings are held to showcase school programs and activities, to provide parent education, or to offer the opportunity to meet other parents (e.g., feature a school activity or project such as the school choir or band, a drama group, science experiments, or technology displays; provide a speaker to present information on a topic of interest to parents such as homework strategies, discipline, or health-related topics; provide a brief information session by the School Council on a topic or issue of current interest to the school community).
- Arrangements are made to have interpreters available for a variety of purposes.

- Classroom and library materials include groups of people of various genders, abilities, socio-economic levels, faith, and ethnocultural backgrounds engaged in a range of positive roles and situations.
- School libraries and classrooms have books in students' languages, as well as dual-language books.
- The arts program exposes students to the works of artists, musicians, and playwrights from a variety of cultures, and provides opportunities for students to express themselves in a variety of artistic forms from other cultures.
- School clubs promote goals of inclusion, humanitarianism, and global citizenship.

For ideas on how to involve the parents of ELLs in School Councils, see "Involving Parents in the School: Tips for School Councils."
http://www.edu.gov.on.ca/eng/parents/involvement/welcomemat.html

What a safe, respectful, and caring school looks like

- School staff practises and uses the correct pronunciation of students' names.
- School staff respects cultural customs and creates opportunities to bridge cross-cultural communication gaps (e.g., acknowledge that in some cultures it may be considered inappropriate for a child to ask for help, express opinions openly, or make direct eye contact with an adult and point out when or why it is appropriate in Canadian society).
- Staff consult their board's multicultural calendar to ensure that major school activities are scheduled on days that do not conflict with religious holidays. See also *www.multiculturalcalendar.com*
- Newcomer students and their families are informed of school safety rules and drill procedures (e.g., fire alarm, stranger alert, lockdown).
- School staff ensures that new ELLs know how to get home safely at the end of the day.
- School staff shows younger ELLs where to meet family members or locate school buses.
- Rules for the use of the playground and playground structures are explained.
- Anti-discrimination, anti-violence, and anti-bullying policies are explained and strategies and resources are shared with newcomer families and students.
- Character education initiatives, anti-litter campaigns, and opportunities to develop social leadership skills are discussed with newcomer families and students.

Cultures have different naming conventions (e.g., order of family name and given name, double family names, different surnames for children and parents due to cultural and faith traditions).

- Multicultural programs and events welcome all parents and provide opportunities to share and enjoy a wide range of traditions, cultures, sports, and other activities (e.g., acknowledge the United Nations day designated to celebrate first languages, run an outdoor recreation day featuring a popular international sport such as cricket, organize family literacy events and use dual-language books).

What a fair and equitable school looks like

- ELLs are represented among students who make school announcements, participate in school plays, and are teacher helpers.
- ELLs are members of school sport teams, clubs, and other extracurricular activities.
- Accommodations and modifications to instructional and assessment strategies appropriate for ELLs are part of every teacher's repertoire.
- Resources specifically suited to English language learners provide equitable access to curriculum.
- Newcomer parents are invited to attend the next School Council meeting, introduced, asked if they need any assistance with information, and are encouraged to attend subsequent meetings.
- There is a School Council display including contact information and a school activities sign-up sheet for parent volunteers.

Orientation information may include the following:
- basic information about the structure of the school day and year
- a description of important school routines (e.g., food-allergy alert, school trips)
- school phone number and names of important contact persons (e.g., the principal, the office administrative assistant, the ESL or ELD teacher, a bilingual contact person, an interpreter, or a school settlement worker)
- a description of the Ontario school system
- information on the role of parents in Ontario schools

Part of the orientation information that parents receive should address policies supporting equity and inclusion that are implemented in schools and contained in the Ontario curriculum.

Insight

Care should be taken not to overwhelm families with too much information all at once. Establish a relationship with the parents so that their orientation to school can continue over time and parents feel welcome to approach the school with questions and concerns.

Orientation is not a one-time event for newcomer families. As differences between the school in the home country and Ontario become apparent, new questions may arise. Parents may also need support in gaining awareness of the complex nature of learning the language of instruction at the same time as their children are learning the curriculum. They need to become aware of how long it takes students to acquire English for everyday and academic purposes. They also need to understand the goals of the ESL and ELD programs, the organization of the programs at the school, and the approaches to instruction and assessment.

ESL and ELD instruction supports student learning in a variety of ways:
- learning the language of instruction;
- integrating academic language and literacy skills in all subjects;
- developing concepts, learning skills, and critical-thinking skills;
- using information technology effectively;
- helping students to become active learners, who take responsibility for their own learning and who participate fully in their classes;
- using information technology effectively.

Approaches to instruction and assessment that may be different from those of an ELL's home country include:
- the importance of oral language as a basis for learning and literacy (e.g., purposeful/ accountable talk);
- the interactive nature of the Ontario classroom (e.g., working with peer partners and in small groups, teacher-student conferences);
- the wide range of instructional strategies involving a variety of learning styles;
- the focus on process (with attention to students' thoughts, reflection, and personal application of new learning), as well as product;
- ongoing assessment used for different purposes – assessment for learning, as learning, and of learning.

Questions parents ask

My daughter is an ESL student. Is she receiving the same education as her peers?

Yes, she is learning the grade-level curriculum. But because she is also learning English, her ESL teacher and I plan how we can best help her learn science, social studies, and the other subjects through accommodations, such as pre-teaching key vocabulary, providing outlines of paragraphs to use when writing, and extra time for classroom tasks.

Sometimes we modify specific curriculum expectations because her current English proficiency prevents her from being able to show all her knowledge and understanding of some new learning. For example, yesterday in science the students were starting to think about ways to conserve energy and deciding which ways they think are best. Your daughter focussed on one way and was able to list the advantages and disadvantages.

As she learns more English, the ESL teacher and I will change the kinds of support she receives.

My child has missed a lot of school on our way to Canada. She can't read and write in our language and does not know English. How will she be able to cope with this grade level?

In Ontario, children are placed in classes with students who are the same age. This allows her to be with children who are at the same social and emotional development level. Because your daughter has some gaps in her education, her ELD program will build on her background knowledge and help her acquire English literacy skills at the same time.

By organizing an uninterrupted block of learning time for your daughter and a small group of other students, we hope to accelerate her learning. It does take time, though, to become comfortable in school and be successful with grade-level curriculum when you've been away from school for as long as your daughter has been.

I worry about my son learning French at the same time as he is learning English. Shouldn't he be concentrating on only one language?

You might think that he would get confused if he learns French at the same time as he is learning English, but, in fact, the opposite is true. Many of the items taught in French may parallel what students are learning in English, so learning French can help to reinforce the English that they are learning. Children who are learning the English language are likely to feel successful since all students in Ontario are learning French as a second language, and the focus is on oral language using practical, everyday French. Students are able to transfer knowledge about how language works and this may contribute to their overall academic success.

Information for parents about helping with homework is available in 15 languages at *www.edu.gov.on.ca/abc123/ eng/tips/homework.html*

There is no one at home who can help my child with homework. What can I do?

Have your child explain an idea or problem to you in your home language. This will give him the chance to show you whether or not he understands the concept, and you can help him clarify his ideas. It will benefit him to be able to explain the concept in your language as well as in English. If he is having trouble explaining it to you in your language, then you can ask me for extra help for your son. If help is needed to do the homework, your child could go to the homework club at the public library or I can help you arrange for a volunteer-tutor from the nearest secondary school.

Additionally, there are some routines that you can help your child establish that don't involve actually helping to do the homework. For example, set up a routine or schedule for homework and provide a well-lit, quiet space away from distractions like TV, music, and siblings.

Initial assessment

School boards will assign staff to assess the English language proficiency of all English language learners. The assessment will include:

- a structured interview to assess oral communication skills (i.e., listening and speaking);
- an assessment of reading comprehension;
- an assessment of student writing;
- an assessment of mathematical knowledge and skills.

English Language Learners/ESL and ELD Programs and Services: Policies and Procedures for Ontario Elementary and Secondary Schools, Kindergarten to Grade 12, 2007, 2.3.1.

ERGO, the ESL/ELD Resource Group of Ontario, has developed a series of initial language assessment tasks. See *http://www.ergo-on.ca/*

An initial assessment can be conducted in many ways. Some boards have centralized facilities where all newcomer students and families go to obtain orientation information regarding schools in Ontario and where the assessment takes place over the span of one day. In other boards, initial assessment is conducted at the school level and can be spread over a period of days.

The initial assessment is an important first step in getting to know the English language learner. It is an opportunity to get a clear picture of the students' educational, cultural, and personal backgrounds, including their individual learning styles and interests.

For more detailed information on initial assessment of students with LPS, refer to *Supporting English Language Learners with Limited Prior Schooling: A Practical Guide for Ontario Educators, Grades 3 to 12,* **2008.**

The initial assessment also serves as a diagnostic assessment of level of achievement in mathematics and level of proficiency in English. Moreover, it can yield valuable information about students' linguistic, academic, and other strengths, interests, and needs, including any Special Education needs.

Initial assessment results need to be recorded and used as a starting point to inform programming for the student. They also need to be communicated to the student, parents, and all staff working with the English language learner.

> **Insight**
>
> To reduce anxiety for both parents and students, establish a comfortable rapport at the outset (e.g., by showing interest in the family's country of origin or culture, asking for assistance in correctly pronouncing the name of the student, posting a welcome poster in a variety of languages, laying out a display of dual-language books).

The initial interview

The initial interview is a significant opportunity for dialogue among the family, the student, and the school. Adequate time should be allocated so all parties can comfortably exchange necessary information and ask appropriate questions. Where possible, the interview should be conducted in the family's home language, with the support of an interpreter or school settlement worker in order to elicit and clearly understand information being shared, as well as to respect family culture and traditions.

Include the parents in the initial interview. Whenever appropriate, direct questions to the student as that allows for informal assessment of the student's ability to meet the demands of everyday conversation in his or her home language and in English. Parents can supplement responses if more details are needed.

> When confidential information is being discussed, the interpreter should be a bilingual teacher, a professional interpreter, or an adult member of the students' family, to facilitate accuracy of translation.
>
> *English Language Learners/ESL and ELD Programs and Services: Policies and Procedures for Ontario Elementary and Secondary Schools, Kindergarten to Grade 12, 2007, 2.8.3.*

It is inappropriate for students to be asked to interpret at an interview.

Some parents may not be accustomed to answering personal questions from school officials or may not understand the purpose of the questions. When asking for detailed and personal information, everyone should be informed that this is for educational purposes, that in Canada such information is protected by the Freedom of Information and Protection of Privacy Act, and will be shared only with personnel approved by the school board.

It is important to be sensitive to the fact that some families and students have experienced recent loss and trauma when they arrive.

Important considerations for the initial interview of newly arrived students

- Students may or may not be fluent and literate in all languages they speak.
- The home language may have been different from the language(s) studied at school.
- The language of instruction may have been different for different subjects studied.
- Assessment of literacy will be most accurate if completed over a period of time and in different contexts.
- Previous schooling (including information about whether the school was in a rural or urban setting, or refugee camp) may have an impact on knowledge and skills in L1.
  - Many countries do not have Kindergarten programs.
  - Children begin formal schooling at different ages in different countries.
  - The school calendar year may be different from that of Ontario schools.
  - Terminology for "grades" may be different (e.g., *Standard, Form, Primary 1, 2, 3*)
  - Class size may have determined the kinds of teaching and learning.
- Students may not have attended school regularly, for a variety of reasons, and may have repeated a grade.

Some newcomer families may have left their last country of residence under conditions of urgency and may not have brought important documents with them, including academic records. Where records are available, be aware that the grading system and passing marks of other countries can vary from those in Ontario. Also, keep in mind that the order in which curricula is organized and presented in other countries could be different from the sequence of the Ontario curriculum.

For some students, an assessment of language and mathematical skills, conducted in the language of prior schooling, may assist with programming considerations.

Be aware that there are international differences in notation, symbols, directionality, and procedural methods. For example, in some systems the comma sign is used to denote a decimal point.

Initial assessment of mathematics

It is often a good idea to begin with an assessment of mathematical knowledge and skills. English language learners may find it easier to display competence with numbers and symbols than with words of a new language. As well, achievement in mathematics can provide a useful indication of a student's general academic background. Ensure that the assessment tool is free of cultural bias both in the content and in the instructions to students. Instructions should be succinct and avoid the use of passive voice or other complex grammatical structures.

Insight

Various materials for initial assessment of mathematics and English language proficiency have been developed by professional associations and school boards across Ontario. Teachers can also adapt classroom materials and grade-level texts for this purpose, being careful to adjust vocabulary and sentence structure, and screen for cultural content that ELLs may not have had the chance to learn.

Suggestions for assessing skills in mathematics
- Begin with counting and simple computation.
- Give students access to manipulatives and geometric shapes.
- Encourage students to skip over items that seem unfamiliar and look for others that they understand.
- Assess a student's knowledge of key concepts and skills in all five strands of the Ontario mathematics curriculum appropriate for the grade level (e.g., if an English language learner is placed age-appropriately in Grade 5 in September, then assess knowledge of the Grade 4 mathematics curriculum. If the student arrives in January, assess some of the mathematical concepts already covered in Grade 5 as well.)
- Accept different ways to show calculations, as long as they yield correct answers.

Insight

Be conscious of how age and fatigue can affect a student's performance on assessment tasks. Gauge the number of tasks and length of time a student is expected to focus accordingly.

Initial assessment of reading and writing

Getting started

(all ELLs start here)

1. Educational background

2. Initial interview

3. Picture response

4. Writing in your language

Able to participate?

No   *Yes*

Early literacy tasks

1. Reading the alphabet

2. Writing the alphabet

3. Colours

4. Alphabet and words

5. Basic vocabulary

ESL or ELD assessment tasks

1. Pre-reading

2. Reading

3. Reading comprehension

4. Writing

Able to participate with ease?

Yes ⟶

No

Initial assessment is complete.

Continue until reading and writing skills in English are determined.

After the assessment

Program recommendations

Ongoing classroom-based assessment

Placement and programming

A student's level of proficiency in English will not influence the choice of grade placement. In elementary schools, English language learners will be placed with an age-appropriate group.

English language learners should be placed in a grade-level or subject-specific classroom for at least part of each day.

English Language Learners/ESL and ELD Programs and Services: Policies and Procedures for Ontario Elementary and Secondary Schools, Kindergarten to Grade 12, 2007, 2.4.2 and 2.4.3.

Programming is key to supporting ELLs in their school environment. Students' academic and social development is enhanced in an environment where they are able to engage in the learning process with peers. Information gathered from academic records, from parents, and through the initial assessment informs programming in the age-appropriate classroom and determines the amount and type of ESL or ELD support.

English language learners have the double challenge of learning the language of instruction while they are learning the grade-level curriculum. When the necessary curriculum accommodations or modifications are in place, students can successfully participate in all content areas even at beginning levels of English proficiency. The practical and interactive nature of some subject areas, such as the arts, health and physical education, and some aspects of science and technology, may make them especially accessible for English language learners.

Some students may arrive with limited prior schooling. With informed and flexible support from the ESL or ELD teacher, where available, and from classroom teachers, learning can be accelerated by building background content knowledge and by supporting language development.

Newcomer families may require explanations to understand school placement and promotion in the Ontario school system.

ESL and ELD programs and delivery models

School boards will implement programs and services that will enable English language learners to continue their education while learning English.

English Language Learners/ESL and ELD Programs and Services: Policies and Procedures for Ontario Elementary and Secondary Schools, Kindergarten to Grade 12, 2.5.1.

In Ontario elementary schools, ESL and ELD support is provided to enable ELLs to fully access the grade level curriculum. Because students spend a portion or all of their day in the regular classroom, the classroom teacher works with a school- or board-designated ESL or ELD expert to plan programs that facilitate English language proficiency. All teachers share the responsibility for the development of the English language skills of their students.

In all situations, English language learners must receive appropriate program support to enable them to participate successfully in Ontario schools. These may include:

- English as a Second Language (ESL) programs, which are for students whose first language is other than English or is a variety of English significantly different from that used for instruction in Ontario schools. Students in these programs have had educational opportunities to develop age-appropriate first-language literacy skills.
- English Literacy Development (ELD) programs, which are for students whose first language is other than English or is a variety of English significantly different from that used for instruction in Ontario schools. Students in these programs are most often from countries in which their access to education has been limited, and they have had limited opportunities to develop language and literacy skills in any language. Schooling in their countries of origin has been inconsistent, disrupted, or even completely unavailable throughout the years that these children would otherwise have been in school. As a result, they arrive in Ontario schools with significant gaps in their education.

English Language Learners/ESL and ELD Programs and Services:
Policies and Procedures for Ontario Elementary and Secondary Schools,
Kindergarten to Grade 12, 2007, 2.5.1. Support material.

ESL and ELD programs are two distinct programs to meet the needs of very different groups of students. ESL programs serve students from Kindergarten to Grade 12. In acknowledging that ELD programs serve students with significant educational gaps, ELD begins in Grade 3, since students will not have had significant gaps if they are in Kindergarten, Grade 1, or Grade 2. ELD programs help students accelerate their learning of content and literacy skills appropriate to their age. They prepare students to transfer to ESL programs where students have age-appropriate literacy skills.

School boards will design programs and services for English language learners so that they are flexible in response to changing needs and reflective of the needs of the students.

English Language Learners/ESL and ELD Programs and Services: Policies and Procedures for Ontario Elementary and Secondary Schools, Kindergarten to Grade 12, 2007, 2.5.3.

Learning a new language for school involves taking many steps on the language acquisition continuum. The length of time to develop the level of proficiency in English that supports academic success will vary from student to student. Therefore, ESL and ELD programs must be flexible to allow for a variety of delivery models, be responsive to learners' changing needs, and to local school circumstances (e.g., distribution and number of English language learners).

Types of support

A variety of support models exists. The support model implemented in a school will be dependent on many different factors, foremost being the number of English language learners in the school, which varies significantly across the province. Some schools have large numbers of ELLs; others have very few. Some schools have ESL or ELD teachers who are on staff for a part or all of every day, while others have itinerant teachers who visit the schools on a regular basis. Some have neither.

Delivery models and support should be flexible and based on the needs of the students. Schools often combine models to suit their populations. What is important is that ELLs need to interact on a daily basis with proficient speakers of English in regular classrooms.

Students' levels of language proficiency determine the type of support required. Though the type of support will change over time, ELLs require a planned support program that endures and may extend to their high school experience.

In an *Integrated Classroom Support* model, the classroom teacher and the ESL or ELD teacher, or the teacher responsible for ELLs collaborate in the planning, instruction, and assessment of grade-level curriculum. The development of language proficiency is tracked through ongoing assessment, which, in turn, determines the scaffolds to instruction, classroom environment, and assessment that need to be in place to support the ELL in classroom learning tasks. The classroom teacher provides targeted instruction specific to the needs of the student through differentiated instruction, either individually or in small groups, as needed.

Tutorial Support may be provided several times per week to small groups of English language learners to provide opportunities for practice and reinforcement of language skills studied in the classrooms. Tutorial work is based on the curriculum units studied in the regular class. Students receive tutorial support, as needed, and continue with further targeted instruction, as required.

Decisions about the way intensive support is delivered need to be made on a child-by-child basis. For beginner ELLs (Stage 1 of Second-Language Acquisition), intensive support will scaffold their learning. When providing intensive support, the teacher works with an individual or a small group of ELLs for an uninterrupted block of time. Students benefit from targeted instruction, integration with their age peers, and literacy learning blocks that focus on both language learning and curriculum. The teacher uses a variety of scaffolds all based on the curriculum units studied in class. Essential critical skills are developed, using modified expectations and accommodations and activities appropriate for individual students. If intensive support is provided through a withdrawal program, these students must be integrated for a portion of the day, and for activities that they can successfully accomplish with their current language proficiency. It is important to ensure that all curriculum areas are being addressed when an ELL is receiving intensive support for English language acquisition.

> It is a challenge for a school to provide programming that meets the distinct needs of English language learners with limited prior schooling. Their needs are very different from those of English language learners who have experienced consistent schooling. These learners share cognitive abilities of their age peers and are keenly aware that they currently lack the skills necessary for success in an academic context.
>
> *Ontario Ministry of Education, Supporting English Language Learners with Limited Prior Schooling: A Practical Guide for Ontario Educators, Grades 3 to 12, 2008, p. 43*

For more detailed information about ELD program delivery models such as *congregated, literacy and numeracy blocks,* and *mathematics and literacy connection*, refer to *Supporting English Language Learners with Limited Prior Schooling, A Practical Guide for Ontario Educators, Grades 3 to 12*, 2008, pp. 43-50.

Monitoring and reporting to parents

> The school board will establish procedures for ensuring ongoing assessment of the development of proficiency in English and the academic progress of each English language learner. Progress will be reported to parents on a regular basis.
>
> **English Language Learners/ESL and ELD Programs and Services: Policies and Procedures for Ontario Elementary and Secondary Schools, Kindergarten to Grade 12, 2007, 2.8.1.**

While the initial assessment provides information for tentative programming, it is important to assess each student's progress on an ongoing basis and to make changes to a student's program as required to increase support, decrease support, or change the type of support.

The information gathered about student achievement needs to be communicated to students and parents in a variety of informal and formal ways, using an interpreter when needed. Ongoing communication about student progress includes information about how the teacher supports the learning of the ELL in the classroom.

> When learning expectations are modified for English language learners, evaluation will be based on the documented modified expectations. This will be noted on the report card and explained to parents.
>
> **English Language Learners/ESL and ELD Programs and Services: Policies and Procedures for Ontario Elementary and Secondary Schools, Kindergarten to Grade 12, 2007, 2.8.2.**

Individual student instruction is modified or accommodated as is necessary, and the supports provided change as language proficiency increases. The kinds of support required for one subject may be different from the kinds of support required for other subjects. Additionally, students may not require support in all subject areas at any given time.

Teachers indicate, by checking the ESL or ELD box on the report card, when modifications to curriculum expectations have been made. The ESL or ELD box on the report card is not checked if modifications have not been made. The box is not checked if accommodations have been provided.

Participation of ELLs in large-scale assessments

Every Ontario student is given the opportunity to participate in large-scale assessments at various points throughout his or her educational career. These may be pan-Canadian assessments, provincial or board based, which are often criterion-based. The purpose of these assessments is to inform teachers about how they can improve instruction to raise the achievement of all students across the province.

Norm-based assessments are often designed for English-speaking children who are familiar with the cultural references contained within the tests. Consequently, the results may solely be an indicator that they are still developing their proficiency in English and are not yet ready to work unsupported in the classroom for some or all of their learning.

The validity of the assessment may be compromised if changes are made to the way the test is either conducted or scored. Careful consideration should be given to decisions about including English language learners in provincial, national, and international large-scale assessments.

ELLs and EQAO testing

English language learners should participate in the Grade 3 and Grade 6 provincial assessments in reading, writing, and mathematics, and in the Grade 9 provincial assessment in mathematics, when they have acquired the level of proficiency in English required for success.

> Decisions about exemptions or deferrals will be made according to the requirements articulated in the EQAO administration guide.
>
> *English Language Learners/ESL and ELD Programs and Services: Policies and Procedures for Ontario Elementary and Secondary Schools, Kindergarten to Grade 12, 2007, 2.9.1 and 2.9.2.*

The EQAO Administration Guide outlines information about exemptions or deferrals of students, including those for English language learners. Additionally, it articulates accommodations for ELLs.

If English language learners were required to write under the same conditions as their English proficient peers, the results could be more influenced by the level of English proficiency than by the literacy skills that those tests were attempting to tap. Furthermore, the results may not be able to show whether the ELL is learning English at the same rate as other ELLs of the same age and same English proficiency, and who have been in Ontario the same length of time.

Insight

EQAO results are reported at the provincial, school board, and school levels. They are used by the Ministry of Education, district school boards, and schools to improve learning, teaching, and student achievement.

Framework: Assessment of Reading, Writing and Mathematics, Junior Division (Grades 4 – 6). Toronto: Education Quality and Accountability Office, 2007

Classroom assessment and English language learners

Many assessment tools require students to read unfamiliar material aloud while the teacher completes a running record of miscue analysis. ELLs are often concentrating more on pronunciation than on comprehension, and may be so anxious about performance that they get little or no meaning from what they are reading aloud. The miscues that they make may relate less to comprehension strategies than they do to the fact that they are struggling to pronounce unfamiliar words in a language in which they are not yet proficient. Further, the content of the reading material may pose a challenge to ELLs who do not share the same background knowledge or cultural interpretation of the material.

Experts tell us

...there is no way to know whether ELLs tested in English score low because of lagging content knowledge and skills, or because of limited English proficiency, or because of other factors that interfere with their test performance – or some combination.

Claude Goldenberg, "Teaching English Language Learners: What the Research Does – and Does Not – Say," American Educator, Summer 2008: 8-23

Discontinuation of ESL or ELD support

English language learners should receive ESL/ELD program support until they have acquired the level of proficiency required to learn effectively in English with no ESL/ELD support.

English Language Learners/ESL and ELD Programs and Services: Policies and Procedures for Ontario Elementary and Secondary Schools, Kindergarten to Grade 12, 2007, 2.10.

Classroom teachers understand that they share the responsibility for supporting English language learners in their goal of achieving language proficiency and in attaining the requisite background knowledge for continued success in learning. Differentiated instruction supports the learning of all students in the class; however, differentiated instruction for ELLs requires additional direct language instruction. As ELLs develop their English-language skills and broaden their knowledge base, teachers work as teams to track and monitor their progress.

The decision about when an English language learner is able to succeed in the classroom without ESL or ELD support is ultimately the responsibility of the principal, in consultation with the student, the parents, and the ESL/ELD and classroom teachers.

The decision to discontinue ESL or ELD support requires a complex examination of a variety of factors that together present a holistic picture of that child. At this point in the student's learning continuum, this decision depends on evidence that the student will be successful within the range of differentiated instruction offered by the classroom teacher.

ELLs with Special Education needs

> School boards will develop a protocol for identifying English language learners who may also have special education needs.
>
> Where Special Education needs have been identified, either in the initial assessment or through later assessments, students are eligible for ESL or ELD services and special education services simultaneously.
>
> *English Language Learners/ESL and ELD Programs and Services: Policies and Procedures for Ontario Elementary and Secondary Schools, Kindergarten to Grade 12, 2007, 2.3.3 and 2.3.4. Support Material.*

Some English language learners have Special Education needs. They are as likely as any other student to be intellectually gifted, to have a learning disability or a behavioural disorder, or even to have multiple exceptionalities.

Many countries around the world have identification and support protocols in place that closely parallel those of Ontario. Others do not. As a result, not all students who have Special Education needs will come with documents similar to psychological assessment reports and/or IEPs, and even if they do, families may not understand when or how to share these with the school.

Ongoing consultation with parents and other school staff including, where available, the ESL or ELD teacher, the Special Education teacher, and the Guidance counsellor, needs to be established as supports for learning are being considered.

It is imperative that English language learners who have exceptionalities be identified as soon as possible so that appropriate programming and placement can be arranged. Students should not be assessed as having learning disabilities on the basis of performance or behaviours that reflect a process of language acquisition or acculturation, or a lack of prior opportunity to acquire the knowledge and skills being tested. English language learners must have equitable access to appropriate programming to ensure that they reach their potential.

The same behaviours in one student may have a different cause than for another. This is especially true in the case of English language learners. Strong similarities of surface behaviours may lead teachers to make incorrect assumptions about their learners. The first step is a careful observation, over time, of what the ELL can do in a variety of classroom activities and settings.

Conclusions must be cautiously drawn to avoid inaccurate labelling of the causes of the behaviours observed in the classroom.

Some potential difficulties related to language learning or to Special Education needs

Observable behaviour	Possible explanation in a language learning context	Possible explanation in a Special Education context
Adds or deletes words; uses known words to replace other words	May not yet know the word; may not have internalized the words or requires more rehearsal of words	Has memory/oral language processing difficulties
Is easily distracted	Doesn't understand; is overloaded with new information; requires more visual/concrete support	Has an auditory processing problem, ADHD, or ADD
Has trouble following directions	Doesn't know the vocabulary in the instructions	Has sequencing or memory problems
Can complete arithmetic calculations but not solve word problems	Doesn't know vocabulary of the word problem; isn't familiar with the currency; has no prior experience with the content	Has processing or abstract reasoning problems; a memory problem; sequencing issue; may not be able to generalize from previous examples
Avoids writing	Lacks confidence or is not comfortable with having multiple drafts of work before the final version	Has fine motor difficulties and limited expressive language
Can't retell a story in sequence or summarize a plot	Is unfamiliar with too much of the vocabulary of the story	Has organization or processing problems

Else Hamayan, Barbara Marler, Cristina Sanchez-Lopez, and Jack Damico. *Special Education Considerationsfor English Language Learners: Delivering a Continuum of Services.* Caslon Publishing, 2007. p.40

Protocols for Assessments

[Assessments] should be administered in the student's dominant language or with the assistance of a bilingual educator, whenever possible. Assessors should use more than one instrument or set of instruments in considering the learning characteristics and describing the performance of English language learners. Assessors should also take into account the student's prior opportunities for learning.

English Language Learners/ESL and ELD Programs and Services: Policies and Procedures for Ontario Elementary and Secondary Schools, Kindergarten to Grade 12, 2007, 2.3.4. Support material

Traditional normed tests, including some psycho-educational assessments, should be used with discretion. They may not garner accurate results since other factors like the familiarity with the vocabulary of the test or culturally specific content could interfere with a student's ability to answer correctly. The valuable feedback from all staff who have worked with the student will assist the IPRC committee in its determination about the Special Education needs of the ELL.

Careful consideration must be made about whether ELLs with Special Education needs should participate in normed tests. The special provisions afforded to all students with Special Education needs may not be sufficient to support the learning needs of this particular subgroup of learners.

Insight

Standardized tests should be used with discretion; cultural and/or linguistic bias in tests may result in unreliable or invalid data.

English Language Learners Student Pre-Referral for Psychological Assessment,
ESL/ELD Resource Group of Ontario, 2008.

ERGO, the ESL/ELD Resource Group of Ontario has developed a three-step protocol for Pre-Referral for Psychological Assessment. Referral to the School Support team is made if the ELL is not progressing in the adapted program. The following four areas are considered:
- a review of student information
- a focus on interpersonal skills
- the collection of information from a various sources
- the consideration of academic progress

For more detailed information, consult English Language Learners Considerations Prior to Referral for Psychological Assessment at *http://www.ergo-on.ca/*

The development of an Individual Education Plan (IEP) for an English language learner needs to take into consideration both the needs related to language learning and the needs related to the student's exceptionality. However, an IEP is a document to support the Special Education needs that exist for the student. It is not a document to describe strategies for the development of English language proficiency. A delicate interplay of Special Education and ESL or ELD supports will provide the structure and scaffolds necessary for the acquisition of English.

Transition from the elementary to the secondary school program

A student entering the Ontario secondary school system at any grade level may count a maximum of 3 ESL or ELD credits as compulsory English credits. (Four compulsory English credits are required for graduation.)

English Language Learners/ESL and ELD Programs and Services: Policies and Procedures for Ontario Elementary and Secondary Schools, Kindergarten to Grade 12, 2007, 2.6.1.

Some newcomer students may first arrive in elementary school in Ontario part way through their Grade 8 year, but many English language learners make the transition to Grade 9 after one or more years in an Ontario elementary school, where a variety of models for ESL and ELD support may be in place. Many of these students are still learning English – especially Academic English – even though they may not have been receiving direct ESL or ELD support in Grade 8. These students will benefit from ESL or ELD credit courses in Grade 9 to help them master the academic language demands of the secondary school program (e.g., understanding English literary devices, making oral presentations in English, and writing reports and essays).

Schools should establish protocols and programs for easing the transition of English language learners from elementary to secondary school.

Transition protocols can include:

- partnerships between elementary and secondary schools that allow older students to share their secondary school experiences with younger children (e.g., homework partners, school ambassadors, cross-curricular community history projects);
- opportunities for students from Grade 8 to explore secondary school options with support from teachers and parents;
- sharing of information with students and parents about the difference in the nature of ESL and ELD support offered by elementary and secondary schools (i.e., secondary school ESL and ELD courses are full-credit courses, and can replace a maximum of three compulsory English credits needed to obtain an Ontario Secondary School Diploma), and the challenges of transition;
- teacher visits from secondary to elementary feeder schools to discuss secondary ESL and ELD courses, confer about incoming Grade 9 students, and discuss appropriate placement;
- use of multilingual resources such as *The Newcomer's Guide to Secondary School in Ontario* to provide information to students and parents.

Insight

The NOW (Newcomer Orientation Week) Program is offered in a number of Ontario school boards, as a supportive transition for newcomer adolescents into secondary schools.

For more information about the NOW program, consult
www.settlement.org/site/ed/guide/videos/now/

3 Adapting the Ontario curriculum for English language learners

Experts tell us

We do not first "learn" language and then later "use" it. Second-language learners do not in any case have the time to study English as a "subject" before they use it to learn other things; they must begin to use it as a medium for learning as soon as they enter school, simultaneously developing their second language hand-in-hand with curriculum knowledge.

Pauline Gibbons, *Scaffolding Language, Scaffolding Learning*, 2002, p. 25

Learning a new language is a lot like learning to play an unfamiliar sport or musical instrument. Time, practice, making and learning from one's errors, and a keen desire to succeed, are all part of becoming proficient in an additional language.

The teacher's role in this complex, interactive process is similar to that of a supportive, intentional coach. The teacher helps all students to learn skills and knowledge within the context of the classroom and the curriculum. New vocabulary and concepts in the Ontario curriculum are a matter of course for all learners, not just for ELLs.

Language is taught explicitly in all subject areas. It is the rich exposure to concepts – through dialogue, media, and discussion – that is at the heart of learning. The teacher holds the responsibility for creating a language-rich environment in which learning becomes accessible to the range of students in the classroom.

English language learners bring their prior knowledge of concepts, as well as prior understanding about how language "works" to the new task of learning English. But language learning is much more than acquiring vocabulary or grammatical structures (the words and mechanics). It is about internalizing, expressing, and connecting new concepts, and also communicating those concepts effectively to others. As with a new sport, there are unfamiliar rules to learn and internalize, new explicit skills to acquire, and much practice needed for those various skills to work together harmoniously and automatically.

Differentiating instruction for English language learners

Teachers must adapt the instructional program in order to facilitate the success of English language learners in their classrooms.

Appropriate adaptations to the instructional program include:
- modification of some or all of the subject expectations so that they are challenging but attainable for the learner at his or her present level of English proficiency, given the necessary support from the teacher;
- use of a variety of instructional strategies (e.g., extensive use of visual cues, graphic organizers, scaffolding; previewing of textbooks, pre-teaching of key vocabulary; peer tutoring);
- strategic use of students' first languages;
- use of a variety of learning resources (e.g., visual material, simplified text, bilingual dictionaries, and materials that reflect cultural diversity);
- use of assessment accommodations (e.g., granting of extra time, oral interviews, demonstrations or visual representations, tasks requiring completion of graphic organizers or cloze sentences instead of essay questions and other assessment tasks that depend heavily on proficiency in English).

While the degree of program adaptation required will decrease over time, English language learners continue to need some level of program support in order to experience school success.

The teacher needs to adapt the program for ELLs as they acquire English proficiency. For English language learners, in the early stages of language acquisition, the teacher needs to modify the curriculum expectations, in some or all curriculum areas. Most ELLs require accommodations for an extended period, long after they have achieved proficiency in Everyday English.

Program adaptations: Modifications and accommodations

English language learners are accomplishing two simultaneous tasks: they are learning the curriculum while also learning the language of instruction. For this reason, differentiation of program for ELLs must take into account the unique needs of this group of learners.

Modifications are changes to the curriculum expectations.

Accommodations are strategies and provisions provided by the teacher to enable students to meet the curriculum expectations. When a student's program is accommodated, the provincial curriculum expectations are not altered.

When deciding upon appropriate accommodations or modifications, teachers need to consider the individual ELL's:
- English language proficiency
- prior knowledge
- learning style
- readiness and interests

Describing language behaviours – What students can do and are learning to do

At the time of publication of this resource, the Ministry is in the process of developing a new set of descriptors for the continuum of development of English language proficiency. Teachers should continue to refer to the stages of second language acquisition and literacy development that are described in *The Ontario Curriculum, Grades 1 – 8: English As a Second Language and English Literacy Development – A Resource Guide,* 2001.

http://www.edu.gov.on.ca/eng/document/curricul/esl18.pdf

For your convenience, these descriptors are included in this resource as an appendix.

The following generalized statements describe language behaviours of English language learners whose development of English language proficiency is being tracked. They illustrate how English language proficiency develops over time and are not meant to be used as descriptors for language proficiency assessment.

ELLs receiving ESL programs and services

	Early beginner level (Stage 1 of Second-Language Acquisition)	Later beginner level (Late Stage 1/early Stage 2 of Second-Language Acquisition)
Listening and Speaking	· learning basic vocabulary and very simple sentence structure; · beginning to communicate in single words and phrases; · often understanding more than they can produce themselves when they are in conversation with a partner who is speaking slowly and clearly.	· increasingly able to communicate and are developing confidence in asking simple questions, initiating and responding to simple statements, and engaging in short exchanges and conversations.
Reading	· learning basic vocabulary and becoming familiar with the conventions of English print; · initially, gaining understanding mainly from illustrations, and progressing to reading high-frequency words, simple sentences, and a variety of adapted simple texts.	· developing the ability to read adapted texts for enjoyment and information; · beginning to use text organization, structural features, and comprehension strategies to locate main ideas and some details.
Writing	· beginning to express themselves in written English; · progressing from labelling and copying and or writing personal information to using images, symbols, and printed words to convey meaning; · starting to write simple sentences.	· developing the ability to write a series of linked sentences around a central idea supported by graphic organizers and using familiar vocabulary.

	Early intermediate level (Stage 2 of Second-Language Acquisition)	Later intermediate level (Stage 3 of Second-Language Acquisition)
Listening and Speaking	· initiating social interaction independently · beginning to participate in academic classroom discussions; · increasingly able to understand main ideas and some details presented orally.	· are fluent in social communication with English-speaking peers and adults, using a variety of communicative strategies · participating in academic classroom discussions with growing confidence · beginning to use vocabulary and sentence structures presented in academic work · comprehending more detailed information on familiar topics presented orally.
Reading	· increasingly able to read a variety of familiar text forms for enjoyment and information; · responding to text with scaffolds provided by the teacher.	· using a variety of reading strategies to comprehend grade-level reading, with consistent support and scaffolding · selecting and reading a wide variety of simply structured text forms for pleasure and academic purposes.

	Early intermediate level (Stage 2 of Second-Language Acquisition)	Later intermediate level (Stage 3 of Second-Language Acquisition)
Writing	· developing the ability to write English for personal and academic purposes, using a variety of forms and a wider range of grammatical structures; · beginning to revise their own work with teacher support.	· expanding their skills and confidence in writing; · using expanded vocabulary; · using a wider range of grammatical structures to express ideas and make connections.

	Early advanced level (Stages 3 - 4 of Second-Language Acquisition)	Later advanced level (Stage 4 of Second-Language Acquisition)
Listening and Speaking	· developing fluency, accuracy, and confidence in using English in a wide variety of social and academic situations; · able to comprehend most details and vocabulary on unfamiliar topics.	· developing a level of English fluency, accuracy, and confidence approximating that of English-speaking peers for most social and academic purposes; · using and understanding grade-appropriate language structures and subject-specific vocabulary; · understanding and responding appropriately to nuances of tone and inflection.
Reading	· able to comprehend a variety of grade-appropriate text forms for personal and academic purposes with increasing confidence and some support; · increasingly able to recognize point of view and understand most cultural references and contexts.	· developing a level of reading comprehension approaching that of most English-speaking peers on a range of grade-appropriate texts; · using a variety of grade-appropriate comprehension strategies and text features for personal and academic purposes; · able to recognize point of view and understand most cultural references in context.
Writing	· developing a high level of competence in writing in English; · independently using key vocabulary presented in academic classroom contexts; · independently using basic age-appropriate grammatical structures to express sequence, causality, hypothesis, and connection – with minor errors; · using a variety of forms for specific purposes and audiences; · elaborating ideas and paraphrasing and summarizing information with increasing accuracy; · self-editing with some effectiveness.	· developing a level of competence in English writing that approaches that of most English-speaking peers; · using a range of grade-appropriate stylistic elements and organizational formats for a variety of personal and academic purposes; · independently using a full range of age-appropriate grammatical structures to express sequence, causality, hypothesis, and connection – with few errors; · writing and editing with an awareness of audience and nuance, reflecting a sense of their own writing voice; · self-editing effectively.

ELLs receiving ELD programs and services

Students who have significant gaps in their education because of limited prior schooling will require different kinds of support than other ELLs. English Literacy Development (ELD) programs, designed to support these English language learners, begin in Grade 3.

Individual students may follow a somewhat different path, but the goal for all students on the ELD continua is eventual transfer to the ESL continua.

	Early beginners (Stage 1 ELD of Second-Language Acquisition)	Later beginners (Stages 1 – 2, ELD of Second-Language Acquisition)
Listening and Speaking	· learning basic vocabulary and very simple sentence structure; · beginning to communicate in single words and phrases; · often understanding more than they can produce themselves when they are in conversation with a partner who is speaking slowly and clearly.	· increasingly able to communicate; · developing confidence in asking simple questions, initiating and responding to simple statements, and engaging in short exchanges and conversations.
Reading	· beginning to decode simple words to read for meaning and are highly dependent on illustrations and graphics that support the text; · progressing to reading high frequency words and simple sentences.	· developing their ability to read adapted texts for enjoyment and information; · using familiar comprehension strategies, including visual cues, prior knowledge, and rereading.
Writing	· learning the English alphabet; · starting to copy and label and, with highly structured scaffolds, progressing to writing simple sentences about familiar topics and experiences.	· developing the ability to write a series of linked sentences around a central idea prompted by sentence starters and using familiar vocabulary, with strong scaffolding by the teacher.

	Early intermediate level (Stage 3 ELD of Second-Language Acquisition)	Later intermediate level (Stage 4 ELD of Second-Language Acquisition)
Listening and Speaking	· developing the confidence to initiate interaction and to participate in classroom discussions; · are increasingly able to understand main ideas and some details presented orally.	· continuing to develop oral fluency in communication with English-speaking peers and adults; · using a variety of communicative strategies, including using pauses, tone and intonation, and facial expressions to emphasize meaning; as well as restating and paraphrasing; · becoming more accurate in word choice and grammatical forms; · demonstrating ability to comprehend more detailed information on familiar topics.

	Early intermediate level (Stage 3 ELD of Second-Language Acquisition)	**Later intermediate level** (Stage 4 ELD of Second-Language Acquisition)
Reading	· expanding their reading skills by reading for enjoyment and information with strong scaffolding; · developing an expanded bank of everyday and basic academic vocabulary.	· increasingly able to read a variety of scaffolded texts in various curriculum areas; · using a variety of reading comprehension strategies to read critically with some confidence.
Writing	· writing short, anecdotal pieces independently; · using a variety of text forms with strong scaffolding; · beginning to revise their own written work independently.	· expanding their skills and confidence in writing for personal and academic purposes; · developing the ability to write a series of linked sentences around a central idea, supported by graphic organizers and using familiar vocabulary; · using expanded vocabulary; · using a range of simple grammatical structures to express ideas and make connections.

Our commitment is to every student. This means both "raising the bar" to encourage the absolute highest achievement from our students and "closing the gap" to ensure that we develop strategies to help every student learn, no matter what their personal circumstances.

Reach Every Student — Energizing Ontario Education, 2008, p. 2

Making language and content accessible for English language learners

It is important for teachers to identify language that may be confusing to ELLs and to substitute clearer alternatives. Students learn language best when they can understand what is said by inference: that is, by making connections to what they already know. To help students do this, teachers can use the following techniques:

- *Simplify vocabulary.* Choose simple, straightforward words that are in everyday use. For example, most students will understand "Learn the new words" more easily than "Review the new vocabulary."

- *Recycle new words.* Reintroduce new words in a different context or use recently learned words to reintroduce or expand a concept.

- *Simplify sentence structure.* Avoid complex sentences and passive verbs if possible. For example, instead of "The homework must be completed and handed in by Friday," it would be better to say "You must finish the work and give it to me on Friday."

- *Highlight key ideas and instructions.* Review instructions and concepts periodically with the class to reinforce students' comprehension. Pause to get students' attention before making an important point, and make sure all students can see you. Use gestures for emphasis, raise pitch and volume slightly, repeat or rephrase (or ask a student to do so).

- *Provide notes that highlight key ideas and new words.* Use the chalkboard or post a chart in the classroom for ongoing reference. Provide a summary sheet so that students can refer to it when studying at home.

- *Give clear, explicit instructions.* Number and label the steps in an activity. Reinforce oral instructions for homework and projects with a written outline to help students who may not be able to process oral instructions quickly enough to understand fully.

- *Use many non-verbal cues.* Gestures, facial expressions, and mime help learners grasp the meaning of what you are saying. Be aware that some gestures (e.g., pointing at people) may have negative meanings in some cultures.

- *Make frequent use of a variety of concrete and visual supports.* These might include models, toys, math manipulatives, pictures, charts, flashcards, vocabulary lists, key visuals, posters, and banners. Demonstrate procedures and provide related hands-on activities.

- *Allow sufficient response time when interacting orally.* Students need time to think in the first language and compose a response in the second.

- *Check often for comprehension.* For example, at frequent intervals say, "Tell me what you have to do next."

- *Provide bilingual support.* For students who are in the early stages of learning English, bilingual peers can clarify instruction, provide translations of key words that are difficult to explain in English, and help to determine whether a student understands.

- *Speak naturally, but pause briefly between phrases.* This gives English language learners time to process the smaller chunks of language. This also helps them recognize English as it is actually spoken.

- *Be conscious of words that need further explanation.* It may be necessary to explain contractions such as "don't" and non-standard spoken forms such as "gonna."

- *Use key visuals.* Key visuals are teacher-developed graphic organizers that show how ideas are related. T-charts, Venn diagrams, flow charts, story maps, timelines, and decision trees are examples of organizers that are not dependent on language knowledge and that promote the development of thinking skills such as classifying, relating cause-and-effect, comparing and contrasting, or following a sequence.

- *Monitor your use of idioms, cultural references, jokes, colloquial forms, figurative language, slang, and unusual idioms.* For example, saying "Run that by me again" or "That answer is in the ballpark" may be confusing. Avoid using slang and unusual idioms with beginning ELLs. With students who have progressed beyond the beginning stage, develop techniques for explaining the use of non-literal expressions, for example, post a list of the week's idioms on a bulletin board.

Adapted from "Supporting ESL/ELD Learners in the Classroom," in *Multilingual Education in North York Schools*, North York Board of Education, 1998, p. 8–9. Used with permission of the Toronto District School Board.

Strategies to support beginning English language learners

Classroom organizational strategies

- Brainstorm with the class ways in which all students can make the classroom a welcoming place.
- Practise and model the correct pronunciation of the student's name.
- Assign buddies, mentors, and peers to support and encourage class participation.
- Seat students where they can hear and see well, and near classmates who will provide support and language modelling.
- Take students on a tour of the school and provide the school's floor plan.
- Gather learning materials that students can use independently or with a buddy, such as picture books with tapes, math activities, interactive CD-ROMs, and word games.
- Label the objects in the classroom environment in English and in the students' first languages.
- Post timetables where students can refer to them.
- Provide key visuals to support themes, and to help bring language to life (e.g., from magazines, newspapers, posters, flyers, the Internet).
- Give newcomer students classroom jobs to perform, to assist with socialization and orientation (e.g., distributing classroom materials, monitoring attendance, going on errands).
- Give students positive feedback for their efforts.
- Demonstrate ways that all students in the class can be helpful to the ELLs.
- Set short-term goals for students based on observations. In the early days after arrival, they might be learning the classroom routines and survival English.
- Find out what the new students' interests are and use this information to create related assignments to engage them and to encourage the learning of English.

- Encourage participation in extracurricular activities as increased opportunities for language acquisition.

Instructional strategies

- Provide bilingual and picture dictionaries and picture cards to assist students in creating their own bilingual dictionary.
- Encourage the use of the first language in journal writing, personal dictionaries, word lists, prewriting activities, and when preparing outlines or drafts.
- Create a word wall (with first language translations) with pictures to introduce and reinforce unit-specific vocabulary, and teach students how to use it as a tool to increase understanding.
- Teach students to use the computer and/or level-appropriate computer software.
- Pre-teach key vocabulary associated with a walking tour of the school community.
- Take students on a walking tour of the school community. Record a language-experience story on chart paper, based on class responses to simple questions about the trip. Ask students to copy the story and then practise reading it aloud to a peer.
- Use desktop picture alphabet charts to aid beginning writers and those whose first language alphabets differ from that of English.
- Model all activities for students.
- Find out about the student's prior knowledge about a topic and use it to make connections and address gaps.
- Allow students to demonstrate their understanding of a concept in alternative ways (e.g., demonstration, speech, picture, writing in the first language).
- Check often for comprehension.
- Give clear instructions (e.g., number and label the steps in an activity).
- Adapt lessons to the individual ELL's level of English proficiency.

Explicit language-teaching strategies

- Simplify vocabulary, using simple, straightforward words that are in everyday use.
- Teach the English for important personal information (e.g., address, phone number).
- Teach key survival phrases such as: "Where is...?", "Hello," and "Goodbye." Use pictures and actions to reinforce meaning.
- Teach essential vocabulary using a variety of supports (e.g., models, charts, pictures, diagrams, word cards, picture books, toys, posters, banners).

- Recycle new words. reintroduce new words in a different context, or use recently learned words to introduce or expand a concept.
- Simplify sentence structure.
- Pre-teach key vocabulary associated with a new assignment or topic.
- Ask bilingual peers and volunteers to help clarify instructions.
- Explicitly teach the Roman alphabet to those students whose first language uses a different alphabet.
- Use real objects to teach vocabulary (e.g., articles of clothing, leaves and acorns, fruits and vegetables).
- Ask students to match pictures to vocabulary or to draw pictures that go with the words.
- Introduce musical chants that reinforce everyday expressions and patterned speech.
- Use themes to develop vocabulary (e.g., the classroom, the school, the family).
- Learn and use words and phrases from the student's first language to clarify instructions and key concepts.

Ongoing strategies for supporting English language learners

Instructional strategies

- Design lessons and activities and choose resources that take into account students' background knowledge and experiences.
- Adapt programs to enable students to be successful. This may include modifications to some of the curriculum expectations and/or accommodations which might include the use of bilingual dictionaries or extra time for completing tests.
- Encourage students to share information about their own languages and cultures to raise awareness for all.
- Allow sufficient response time when students are interacting orally with the English language.
- Demonstrate procedures and provide related hands-on activities.
- Use graphic organizers to show how ideas are related. T-charts, Venn diagrams, flow charts, story maps, and timelines are examples of organizers that are not dependent on language knowledge and that promote the development of thinking skills, such as classifying, relating cause and effect, comparing and contrasting, or following a sequence.
- Design all lessons to include a component which activates prior knowledge (e.g., K-W-L chart, brainstorming) and a review of key concepts).
- Encourage ELLs to ask for assistance from peers.

- Chunk information by breaking tasks down into smaller, more manageable pieces.
- Provide feedback on one kind of error at a time. Note specific, habitual errors and provide direct instruction later.
- Select common errors as the language feature of the week, teach them explicitly, and provide opportunities for practice.
- Encourage ELLs to keep an editing checklist containing examples of errors and corrections, for their reference.
- Give clear directions. Explain them explicitly. Assign one step at a time, allowing students to complete each step before introducing another. Further reinforce directions by writing them on the board or on chart paper.
- Model the process and the product.
- Provide multiple opportunities for practice.

Explicit language teaching strategies

- Use subject content as a vehicle for English-language instruction. Provide students with opportunities to acquire language in a context that is interesting and relevant to encourage and enhance language learning.
- Highlight the ways in which language is used in specific subject areas to assist students in acquiring the specialized vocabulary and language skills appropriate to each discipline. For example, in science and technology, students need practice in using the passive voice to write reports or describe processes. In mathematics, students need to understand and use expressions for comparing quantity, speed, and size, as well as the words and phrases related to mathematical operations.
- Recycle new words, reintroduce new words in a different context, or use recently learned words to introduce or expand a concept.
- Encourage students to retell instructions in their own words.
- Have students review main concepts and vocabulary with partners in a Think-Pair-Share task and in whole-class sessions at the end of each lesson or activity.
- Teach language structures by highlighting specific structures (e.g., the imperative, the simple present), using a variety of strategies, such as flashcards, repetition, role play, charts with pictures, and guided writing.
- Make all students aware of phonetic structures through think-aloud questions (e.g., "What sound does classroom begin with?").
- Point out contextual clues that help students with meaning. For example, in mathematics, words such as area, table, and into have a different meaning from their everyday meaning.
- Have students create subject-specific bilingual dictionaries for mathematics and science and technology.

- Provide writing prompts to help students complete specific tasks (e.g., for letter writing).
- Provide writing scaffolds, such as the cloze procedure, to help students use new words and phrases, and to produce sentences, paragraphs, and other forms of writing at a more sophisticated level.
- Use guided reading strategies in which prompts are used to encourage the students to use reading strategies to deepen comprehension.

See *Supporting English Language Learners with Limited Prior Schooling: A Practical Guide for Ontario Educators, Grades 3 to 12,* 2008, for additional strategies that are specifically designed for the English language learner with ELD needs.

Assessment

Through assessment, teachers gather information about their students' prior knowledge, language needs, and learning progress. The educational strengths and needs of ELLs can be identified most effectively through multiple forms of assessment.

Because language learning is developmental and involves experiment and approximation, the educational strengths and needs of ELLs can be identified most effectively through the use of a variety of assessment tools. Teachers should provide students with a wide range of opportunities to demonstrate what they know and what they can do.

Assessment of English language learners should:
- focus on improving student learning;
- be linked directly to curriculum expectations (as modified for each ELL's degree of English language proficiency);
- recognize linguistic and academic progress, while taking into account realistic and varying rates of second-language learning;
- incorporate student self-assessment;
- actively involve students and parents.

To determine if their assessment procedures for ELLs are appropriate, teachers should consider:
- Do assessments reflect appropriate program adaptations?
- Are assessments based on clear statements of expectations?
- Do assessments take into account the student's developing understanding of English?
- Do assessments take into account the cultural and linguistic background of the student?
- Do assessments allow for the use of the student's first language as appropriate?
- Do assessments include clear guidelines for program monitoring?

ELLs bring a wealth of prior knowledge and experience that, when tapped, enriches the knowledge and understanding of all learners in the classroom.

Assessment *for* learning

See *TIPS for English Language Learners in Mathematics*, Ontario Ministry of Education, 2006.

Assessment *for* learning is assessment that informs instruction. Teachers gather information about their students' prior knowledge and language learning proficiency. They can monitor the ELL's progress while targeting and modifying instruction to support the individual's needs.

Some tools and strategies:
- anecdotal records of teacher observation;
- anticipation guides;
- cloze exercises;
- demonstrations or experiments;
- problem solving;
- sequence or matching exercises;
- interactive journals;
- interviews or surveys.

[handwritten note: assessing prior knowledge in order to plan program]

[handwritten note: ① FOR]

Assessment *as* learning

Assessment *as* learning is focussed on th[e] ... [interactive] processes by which students reflect on and make meaning from new information. Teacher monitoring and feedback guides and supports students' learning as ELLs build on prior knowledge, develop critical literacy skills, and set personal learning goals that are developmentally appropriate.

[handwritten note: (FORMATIVE ASSESSMENT)]
[handwritten note: – monitoring ongoing progress towards curriculum expectations]
[handwritten note: – conferencing, – portfolios, – self-assess, – feedback ② AS]

[In p]articular, conferencing is a very effective way of allowing them to [shar]e their understanding and demonstrate their acquisition of the [a]nd skills outlined in the curriculum expectations. Use conferencing [to ...] how well students are progressing toward achieving the [...], and make adjustments as necessary.

[An]d maintaining a portfolio of student work is an excellent way [to ...] demonstrate a student's progress over time. Portfolios allow [... to] see various stages of work in progress and help them begin to [... qu]ality work. Writing portfolios can offer students insight into the [... wr]iting. As well, this information is easily shared with parents to [...] progress.

Some tools/strategies:
- student-teacher conferences;
- portfolio assessment;
- teacher observations (ongoing);
- direct and timely feedback from the teacher;
- peer feedback;
- self-assessment checklist;
- reflective journal entries;
- paragraph frames to guide reflection.

– summative evaluation of evidence of achievement of curriculum expectations

③ OF

Assessment *of* learning

Assessment *of* learning has a summative purpose and uses a collection of evidence to evaluate each student's achievement of curriculum expectations. It is used for reporting to students and parents.

Assessment of learning for ELLs should:
- be based on clear statements of expectations;
- take into account the cultural and linguistic background of the student;
- allow for the use of the student's first language as appropriate;
- include clear guidelines for program monitoring;
- reflect appropriate program adaptations.

Teachers should adjust their expectations according to the length of time students have been in Canada, students' previous educational and social experiences, and the amount of cultural adjustment required. Evaluation procedures should be clear and purposeful and should distinguish between ELL needs and program content needs.

Some tools/strategies:
- portfolio assessment;
- oral reports or presentations;
- retellings;
- journals;
- role plays or simulations;
- demonstrations/experiments;
- peer teaching (e.g., students teach a skill or idea to a peer);
- tests in which the language requirements for understanding and expressing content knowledge have been reduced, appropriate to the student's current degree of English language proficiency;
- rubrics, including those modified for ESL or ELD.

Sample adapted unit frameworks

Three unit frameworks, one at each of the primary, junior, and intermediate divisions, are provided as examples of planning differentiated instruction for ELLs. Each framework follows the process of *planning with the end in mind.* Special consideration was given to the following:

- *Cross-curricular connections* – Clustering expectations helps teachers plan to teach a number of expectations in one unit and to make connections among several subject areas.

- *Prior knowledge and skills* – ELLs bring with them a wealth of educational and life experiences. Making connections between their prior knowledge and the content of the curriculum helps them build on what they already know and succeed in the tasks.

- *Assessment* – Multiple opportunities and methods of assessment have been specifically designed to inform teachers' instruction and students' learning.

- *Meeting the needs of all learners* – ELLs are working toward achieving the same grade level expectations as their peers. Teachers can help them meet the expectations through differentiated instruction.

- *Modification of specific expectations* – Modifications are necessary for some ELLs. Modifications are appropriate when learners are in the early stages of learning English or for when they have had limited prior schooling.

These models of lesson plans for Grades 2, 5, and 7 are snapshots of several lessons in a unit, including the culminating activity. The sample lessons model the processes of adaptation – both modification of expectations and accommodations – required by English language learners at various stages of language proficiency. For each unit, there is a student who is just beginning to learn English, one who is developing, and one who is fairly advanced in his or her knowledge of the language of instruction. Also included in some of the profiles are students who have had limited prior schooling. Modifications and accommodations are provided for the sample students. Teacher Reflections model the ways teachers focus on the expectations of their subjects and develop the necessary scaffolds to support students in meeting the curriculum.

The planning template

Although all units are formatted using a similar template, this is only one example of a template that could be used during the design-down planning done by teachers. There are many well-structured templates available in the field.

The planning template is organized to identify the accommodations and modifications for ELLs throughout the unit. The three columns below show the differentiated tasks for all the learners in the classroom: the left column refers to all the learners in the classroom, the middle three columns focus on differentiation for the ELLs, and the right column includes notes on items that the teacher needs to consider when planning and teaching the unit.

Unit planning template (sample)

Unit overview		
Title		**Grade(s)**
Summary of unit		
Scope and sequence		
Big ideas		
Focus questions		
Overall expectations		
Specific expectations		**Specific expectations (Modifications)**

Assessment and evaluation		
Assessment for learning	*Assessment as learning*	*Assessment of learning*

Links to prior knowledge and skills	

Instructional Activities	Modifications/Accommodations for ELLs			Teacher Considerations
	(ELL and stage)	(ELL and stage)	(ELL and stage)	

Sample adapted unit framework for Grade 2: Movement – Simple machines

Mr. Ramon is a Grade 2 classroom teacher with a diverse group of learners that include 3 ELLs: Hei, Samiya, and Curtis. He is ready to begin a science and technology unit with cross-curricular connections to language. The unit builds on prior experiences and provides connections to the students' lives outside the classroom and is especially suited to hands-on learning.

In planning this unit, Mr. Ramon is careful to consider the learning styles, readiness, and interests of all his students, including ELLs. He works collaboratively with other teachers, including his grade-partner and the ESL teacher.

ESL	ESL	ESL
Hei, Grade 2, Beginner (Stage 1 of Second-Language Acquisition)	**Samiya, Grade 2, Intermediate** (Stage 2 of Second-Language Acquisition)	**Curtis, Grade 2, Advanced** (Stages 3 – 4 of Second-Language Acquisition)
Hei arrived in Canada in November with her parents and two older siblings. In her country of origin, there is no mandatory Kindergarten program. She had completed several months of Grade 1 in her country of origin and was placed age-appropriately in Grade 2 upon arrival in Canada. She can recognize familiar words in her home language (which uses an alphabet different from that of English). She can count and write numerals to 100 in her home language and has started adding and subtracting with single digits using regrouping. Hei is enthusiastic about attending school. In her country of origin, she enjoyed activities involving music, singing, and dancing, and hopes to pursue these interests in Canada.	Samiya has recently arrived in Ontario with her mother and brother. Samiya's father has remained temporarily in his family's country of origin but will arrive to rejoin the family next year. Samiya has received age-appropriate education and has been studying English as a foreign language since Grade 1. She is an avid reader in her first language, and her mother has kept a portfolio documenting her numerous academic awards and achievements in her country of origin (e.g., class newsletter contributions, awards for mathematical excellence). Samiya takes the initiative to ask questions for clarification. She reads and understands short texts in English and can write short sentences. Samiya enjoys using the computer at home.	Curtis was born in Canada, and speaks a language other than English at home with his extended family and in the community. His grandmother looks after Curtis at her house while his parents are at work. Curtis does not often initiate conversation at home in his first language, although he will respond to direct questions from family members in a mix of English and L1. The only language he has been taught to read and write is English. His oral fluency makes some of the teachers in his school surprised to learn that he is receiving ESL support. His classroom teacher and the ESL teacher work with Curtis to help him develop reading comprehension and writing strategies. Curtis enjoys working by himself and loves drawing, especially action figures. He is fascinated by how things work.

Unit overview			
Title	*Simple machines*	**Grade(s)**	2

Summary of unit

Students explore simple machines and a variety of toys that incorporate them. They plan and build as a class a moveable toy that includes at least one simple machine prior to planning and building their own toy. The students analyze an advertisement for a toy before writing one for their newly designed toy.

Scope and sequence

The following list outlines all components of the unit. Three components (marked ★) are later presented in detail to illustrate planning to adapt instruction for English language learners. (Note that lessons will be of varying lengths, and individual lessons may be carried out over a period of several days.)

Planning with the end in mind

- ■ **Culminating task – Plan, build, and advertise a new toy ★**
  - Design a moveable toy that includes at least one simple machine.
  - Build the toy.
  - Create an advertisement for the toy.
  - Display the toy in the classroom.

- ■ **Lesson 5 – Shopping for toys ★**
  - Examine toy ads and identify the important elements (e.g., information, design, and appeal).
  - Look at a picture of a new toy and discuss the elements that could be included in an ad for the toy.
  - Create an ad for the toy.

- ■ **Lesson 4 – How to design and build a toy**
  - Work with the teacher and the whole class to design and build a toy which has moveable parts and uses one or more simple machines.
  - Participate in a modelled writing lesson that recounts the planning and building of the toy.

- ■ **Lesson 3 – Simple machines and how they work**
  - Identify simple machines (mechanisms) found in a home or classroom.
  - Identify and explore six simple machines that help toys move.
  - Begin a personal dictionary that highlights the vocabulary associated with simple machines.

- ■ **Lesson 2 – Introduce simple machines ★**
  - Identify and recall items on a table.
  - Contribute to the creation of a word chart for the unit.
  - Listen to a book about simple machines and make connections to items on the table.

- ■ **Lesson 1 – How can we move things?**
  - Take digital photos of moving and non-moving objects on a school walkabout.
  - Categorize digital photos based on the different ways we can use simple machines.

Big ideas

- Movement is a change in position of an object. (Overall expectations 2 and 3)
- Simple machines help objects to move. (Overall expectations 1, 2, and 3)
- Mechanisms are made up of one or more simple machines. (Overall expectation 2)
- Simple machines and mechanisms make life easier and/or more enjoyable for humans. (Overall expectation 1)

Focus questions

- How do you and your family use simple machines every day?
- How do simple machines help things move?

Overall expectations

Science and Technology

- Assess the impact on society and the environment of simple machines and mechanisms.
- Investigate mechanisms that include simple machines and enable movement.
- Demonstrate an understanding of movement and ways in which simple machines help to move objects.

Language
Oral communication

- Listen in order to understand and respond appropriately in a variety of situations for a variety of purposes.
- Use speaking skills and strategies appropriately to communicate with different audiences for a variety of purposes.

Writing

- Generate, gather, and organize ideas and information to write for an intended purpose and audience.

Media literacy

- Identify some media forms and explain how the conventions and techniques associated with them are used to create meaning.

Unit overview	
Specific expectations	**Specific expectations (Modifications)**
Science and Technology	
2.2 Investigate and describe different types of movement. Identify the six basic types of simple machines – lever; inclined plane; pulley; wheel and axle, including gear; screw; and wedge – and give examples of ways in which each is used in daily life to make tasks easier.	2.2 Hei: Investigate and identify three or more different types of movement by labelling pictures. Samiya and Curtis: Modification of this expectation is not necessary. Accommodations outlined in this unit will support their learning. (Note: Accommodations *are found in the individual lessons provided* as part of this sample unit.)
2.3 Investigate the structure and of simple machines.	2.3 Modification of this expectation is not necessary for these ELLs. Accommodations outlined in this unit will support their learning.
2.5 Use appropriate science and technology vocabulary, including *push, pull, beside, above, wheel, axle,* and *inclined plane,* in oral and written communication.	2.5 Hei: Use some of the appropriate science and technology vocabulary, such as *push, pull, beside, above, wheel, axle,* and *inclined plane,* in oral and written communication. Samiya and Curtis: Modification of this expectation is not necessary. Accommodations outlined in this unit will support their learning.
3.3 Identify the six basic types of simple machines – lever; inclined plane; pulley; wheel and axle, including gear; screw; and wedge – and give examples of ways in which each is used in daily life to make tasks easier.	3.3 Hei: Identify three or more simple machines, such as *lever, wheel,* and *screw,* and give a real-life example. Samiya and Curtis: Modification of this expectation is not necessary. Accommodations outlined in this unit will support their learning.
Language	
Oral communication	
1.2 Demonstrate an understanding of appropriate listening behaviour by using active listening strategies in a variety of situations.	1.2 Hei: Demonstrate an understanding of appropriate listening behaviour by using some active listening strategies when working in a small group, supported by the teacher. Samiya and Curtis: Modification of this expectation is not necessary for these ELLs. Accommodations outlined in this unit will support their learning.
1.6 Extend understanding of oral texts by connecting the ideas in them to their own knowledge and experience; to other familiar texts, including print and visual texts; and to the world around them.	1.6 Hei: Understand oral texts by connecting the ideas in them to her own knowledge and experience. Samiya and Curtis: Modification of this expectation is not necessary for these ELLs. Accommodations outlined in this unit will support their learning.
2.2 Demonstrate an understanding of appropriate speaking behaviour in a variety of situations, including paired sharing and small- and large-group discussions.	2.2 Hei: Demonstrate an understanding of appropriate speaking behaviour when working with a supportive partner and in small-group discussions, supported by the teacher. Samiya: Demonstrate an understanding of appropriate speaking behaviour in a variety of situations, including paired sharing and small-group discussions; in large-group discussions when supported by the teacher. Curtis: Modification of this expectation is not necessary for this ELL. Accommodations outlined in this unit will support his learning.

Unit overview	
Media literacy	
3.4 Produce media texts for specific audiences, using a few simple media forms and appropriate conventions and techniques.	3.4 Modification of this expectation is not necessary for these ELLs. Accommodations outlined in this unit will support their learning.

Assessment and evaluation

Assessment for learning	*Assessment as learning*	*Assessment of learning*
• anticipation guide • peer feedback • teacher observations (ongoing) • student-teacher conferences • ongoing, direct, and timely feedback from the teacher	• peer assessment	• teacher-created rubrics

Links to prior knowledge and skills

| Students may have first-hand experience or knowledge about one or more of the following:
• identifying and using machines
• identifying and using toys
• understanding elements of design
• interpreting advertisements and their purpose
• creating rubrics based on success criteria | Students may have acquired the following skills before beginning this unit:
• providing peer feedback
• revising own work based on feedback
• using and reading an anticipation guide
• identifying the purpose and audience, as well as interpreting the messages, of media text |

Instructional Activities	Modifications / Accommodations for ELLs			Teacher Considerations
	Hei (Beginner ESL –Stage 1)	**Samiya** (Intermediate ESL – Stage 2)	**Curtis** (Advanced ESL – Stages 3 - 4)	

LESSON 2 – INTRODUCE SIMPLE MACHINES

What did you see?

• At the classroom science centre, display a collection of items (or pictures) that are related to the book that will be read aloud. This collection may include items such as a fork, scissors, window blinds, a toy crane, a door stop, a rolling pin, a fan, a ramp, a dump truck, a light bulb, or a jar with a lid. • Children look at the items or pictures for a few minutes. • Cover the items with a cloth. • The children work in partners to identify as many of the items as they can remember. • Ask each pair, in a large group, to identify an item from the table. Record the items on a class chart. Continue with this task until all of the items on the table have been identified. • Post the completed chart on a classroom wall for use during this unit.	Pair Hei with a carefully chosen partner - if possible, one who speaks the same home language.	Confirm that Samiya and Curtis have the vocabulary and correct pronunciation for the items and pictures on the table.		A letter to parents sent home at the beginning of the unit will note the importance of parents' talking to their children in English or their home language about the concepts and vocabulary that the children will learn in this unit. During the activity, circulate around the room to check in with all pairs. It might be necessary to assist Hei's group with the identification and labelling of the items and pictures. This activity would be an ideal time to have the ESL/ELD teacher in the classroom to work with Hei and her partner. It may be necessary to explicitly teach some of the words required to complete this task. The class will continue to develop this word chart as the unit evolves.

Assessment for learning

Students independently complete a short anticipation guide prior to the read-aloud.	Hei and Samiya will complete the anticipation guide in a small group of students led by the teacher.		Curtis will read the anticipation guide with a partner before completing it independently.	This anticipation guide will help the teacher identify vocabulary and concepts that need highlighting during the read-aloud.

Read-aloud

Read a book about simple machines. Make connections between the items and pictures from the table and the simple machines in the text.	Make sure that Hei and Samiya are seated so that the book, words, and pictures are immediately visible to them. Hei and Samiya will need to hear this book several times in order to reinforce the new vocabulary. The ESL teacher (or a parent volunteer) could read it and help them match the items on the table with the illustrations in the book.		Since Curtis is interested in how things work, be sure to include him in the conversation through questioning.	When selecting a text to read to the whole class, consider the literacy and reading levels of ELLs, the amount of new or challenging vocabulary, how engaging the text is, cultural biases, and how supported the text is by visuals. While reading, support comprehension by stopping to make connections, answering questions, and explaining new vocabulary.

Instructional Activities	Modifications / Accommodations for ELLs			Teacher Considerations
	Hei (Beginner ESL – Stage 1)	**Samiya** (Intermediate ESL – Stage 2)	**Curtis** (Advanced ESL – Stages 3 - 4)	
LESSON 5 – SHOPPING FOR TOYS				
• In small groups, students examine a series of ads for manual (non-battery operated) toys. Each group identifies two or three ads that they find most appealing and discuss why. • Guide the discussion to elicit the qualities of the ad that make it appealing. What information in the ad tells us about how the toy is able to move? • Ensure that the students have considered the elements of the design, such as colours, size, images, and information when selecting ads. • List and illustrate the elements on chart paper, creating a design elements chart, for class reference.	Hei selects an ad that she likes and responds to simple questions, focussing on colours, size, and image. (e.g., "What do you like about this ad?", "Which picture do you like best?", "Tell me about the picture.").	Samiya is able to express her ideas about an appealing ad when she is given vocabulary for line styles (*bold*, *thin*, *dotted*, *wavy*); shape names (*triangle*, *balloon*, *silhouette*); and colours (*robin's egg blue*, *navy blue*, *cream*).	Curtis can be challenged through higher order questions such as "Why did you find this ad most appealing?", "What makes your ad different from the others?", "What elements do you see in this ad?"	Introduce appropriate vocabulary to Hei, Samiya, and Curtis as they complete this task. This will help them to express their ideas with more accuracy.
• Display a toy or group of toys. • Students can investigate all sides of a toy as well as its inner workings. • Students work with a partner to complete an ad for the toy. • The groups should include as many of the identified design elements as possible.	Remind Hei and her partner to look at the design elements chart when creating their design.			The design elements chart will support all learners when creating their ads, but the visuals will help Hei use the new vocabulary.
Assessment as learning Students exchange their draft ads with another partner group and use the design elements chart when providing feedback on a checklist. **Assessment for learning** Each partner group uses the peer feedback to revise the ad and produce a final copy.	Meet with Hei and her partner when they are completing the checklist for another group. This discussion will help Hei understand the feedback she will receive about her own design.			Design the checklist to match the elements of design chart so that the ELLs will be able to refer to it when providing feedback.

Instructional Activities	Modifications / Accommodations for ELLs			Teacher Considerations
	Hei (Beginner ESL –Stage 1)	**Samiya** (Intermediate ESL –Stage 2)	**Curtis** (Advanced ESL –Stages 3 - 4)	
CULMINATING TASK – PLAN, BUILD, AND ADVERTISE A NEW TOY				
• Introduce the culminating task to the students and lead the class in a discussion about criteria of a successful toy and an advertisement for one. • With the students, review the teacher-created rubrics that will be used when assessing the toy and advertisement. • Students work independently to design a moveable toy that includes at least one simple machine. They create a labelled design plan of their new toy. • The students make a list of the materials that they need to create the toy. • Conference with each student to discuss the design plan and materials. Modify the plan with the student, if necessary. • Students collect the materials and build the toy.	Hei can begin the plan for her toy by drawing it and then working with a partner or teacher to label her diagram. She will refer to the word chart and her personal dictionary for help with identifying the simple machines and locating words that describe movement. Hei will draw the items on her materials list. Help her label the list. Hei will benefit from being asked specific questions about her labelled design plan (e.g., "What does the lever do?", "Show me the pulley," "Where is the axle?"). Hei will need frequent opportunities to describe the building of her toy.	Samiya can design her toy independently. She should use a picture dictionary to label her toy and create a list of the materials that she needs. Samiya will provide an oral step-by-step description of how she will build her toy.	Curtis is able to complete the plan and materials list independently. During his conference, confirm his use of appropriate academic language for the labelled design of his toy and his plans for building it (e.g., "I need to put a lever here to lift the car and pull it up."). Explain this task using familiar language.	Explain this task using familiar language. Students discuss what kinds of moveable parts and simple machines can be included in their toy. Remind all the students to bring materials (e.g., tissue and cereal boxes, toilet rolls, juice cans, cartons, plastic bottles and containers, lids) to the school to be shared when making the toys. The materials required for this task may not be available in the homes of some ELLs. It is important that all students in the class have access to the materials they need to be successful.
Create an advertisement for the toy. Display the toy with the advertisement in the classroom.	Review the elements of the design chart with Hei. She will require support putting her ideas into writing on the advertisement.	Samiya will use the advertisement created with her partner in Lesson 5 as a model for appropriate language.	Curtis may need focus ed support with writing conventions, spelling, and word choice.	
Assessment of learning Evaluate student achievement using a teacher-created rubric.	Use the modified expectations identified in this unit when creating rubrics for assessing Hei and Samiya's achievement.		Modification of expectations was not necessary for Curtis. Use the class rubric when assessing Curtis' achievement.	If specific expectations have been modified for ELLs, the assessment tool needs to align with the modifications.

Sample parent letter
(to be translated into all home languages)

[date]

Dear Parents/Guardians,

This letter is to inform you that during Term 3, our class will be studying how simple machines move.

To help us with this study, we invite parents/guardians to:

- send flyers with your child that advertise toys in your home language;
- send a (non-battery operated) toy with moving parts. Please make sure that your child's name is on the toy. The toy will be returned home at the end of our study. If your child does not bring a toy from home, there will be a selection of toys available in the classroom that your child may choose from to work with throughout this unit of study.
- send in any recycling items that can be used for building (e.g., tissue boxes, paper rolls, juice cans, paper, cartons);
- talk with your child in your home language about the unit we are doing in class – he/she can point out the *hinges*, *levers*, *wheels* that are on toys or simple machines.

Please make sure that the flyers, toys, and recycling items come to school by Friday of next week.

By responding to this request, your child will be able to build a simple machine/toy at the end of our study.

Thank you for your support.

Sincerely,

Grade 2 teachers

Sample adapted unit framework for Grade 5: Early Civilizations – A museum of innovations

Mr. Mitchell is a Grade 5 classroom teacher with a group of energetic students that includes many ELLs. Among them are three students – Benjime, Min-su, and Olesya. Mr. Mitchell has planned a unit focussing on innovations as part of his class' study of early civilizations. The class has already investigated other aspects of two early civilizations in terms of environments, political and economic systems, leisure activities, values and beliefs, and social structures. They will learn about different innovations of these civilizations and how they have influenced modern society. The tasks leading to the culminating task for this unit will help the students make important connections between early civilizations and their lives today.

The following unit framework includes opportunities for making cross-curricular connections, meeting a range of expectations, and addressing different learning styles. The unit was planned in collaboration with the itinerant ESL/ELD teacher who works with the ELLs two times per week. The unit reinforces skills (e.g., research skills, making notes, summarizing) that some of his students were introduced to during their study of medieval society in Grade 4. Mr. Mitchell's unit provides opportunities to make connections with the prior knowledge and experience of all the learners in his classroom. When planning, he is careful to consider the needs of all learners, including the ELLs.

ESL	ESL	ESL
Benjime, Grade 5, Beginner (Stage 1 ELD of Second-Language Acquisition)	**Min-su, Grade 5, Intermediate** (Stage 2 of Second-Language Acquisition)	**Olesya, Grade 5, Advanced** (Stage 4 of Second-Language Acquisition)
Benjime arrived in Canada one month ago. Prior to coming to Canada, he attended school sporadically because of political instability in his country of origin. He communicates in English using single words and gestures. Benjime enjoys animals and nature and likes looking through the books that his teacher has selected for him. He has quickly learned the English alphabet and is beginning to recognize and copy a few familiar words such as classroom objects, colours, and numbers. Benjime enjoys drama and likes to observe his classmates during role play activities.	Min-su arrived in Canada a few months ago. He lives with his parents and younger sisters. He has age-appropriate literacy skills in L1. He studied English in his country of origin and is able to talk about topics that he has learned. Min-su enjoys reading adventure stories in L1 during his free time. He writes simple stories, journal entries, and email messages using familiar vocabulary. He uses a bilingual learner dictionary independently. Min-su eagerly participates in classroom activities and uses short sentences to communicate ideas. He reads some material independently but requires support with unfamiliar vocabulary. He learns best when information is supported by visuals. Min-su enjoys interacting with his friends who speak his home language and often spends recess playing with them.	Olesya speaks a variety of English that differs from the English of classroom instruction. She has been living in Canada for three years. She lives with her mother and her brother. Olesya is able to lead and participate in small group discussions. She uses a variety of reading strategies to help her determine the meaning of grade-appropriate text. Olesya often requests assistance with organizing ideas and using standard English grammar in her written work. She is an active member of the martial arts club at school and enjoys performing for her peers. Olesya has begun training to become a "playground peacemaker."

Unit overview			
Title	*Early civilizations – A museum of innovations*	**Grade(s)**	5

Summary of unit

Students explore innovations of early civilizations. They choose one innovation and conduct research to demonstrate how it has influenced life today. Students will create an artefact and participate in a classroom "Museum of Innovations."

Scope and sequence

The following list outlines all components of the unit. Three components (marked ★) are later presented in detail to illustrate planning to adapt instruction for English language learners. (Please note that lessons will be of varying lengths, and individual lessons may be carried out over a period of several days.)

Planning with the end in mind

- ■ **Culminating Task – "Museum of Innovations"**
  - Set up the exhibits.
  - Present to own class. ★
  - Make a summary of the innovations of another civilization (based on other groups' presentations).
  - Present the artefact and research to other classes and visitors.

- ■ **Lesson 5 – Plan the presentation**
  - Participate in a lesson on making an effective presentation and create a checklist to be used for assessment.
  - Use the information gathered on the organizer to prepare the presentation.
  - Plan the display with members of the assigned group.
  - Review and edit the presentations with support from group members.

- ■ **Lesson 4 – Conduct individual research ★**
  - Choose one innovation from the assigned civilization.
  - Locate and gather information using an organizer.
  - Design and construct a model of the artefact.

- ■ **Lesson 3 – The research process**
  - Participate in teacher demonstration of what appropriate information is, where to find it, and how to write it in own words.
  - Demonstrate completing the research organizer.

- ■ **Lesson 2 – Explore innovations of early civilizations**
  - Placemat: Generate a list of innovations from civilizations previously investigated (e.g., China: compass, wheelbarrow, abacus).

- ■ **Lesson 1 – Introduction ★**
  - Activate prior knowledge – Yes/No Chart.
  - Mystery Box: Examine contemporary artefacts and discuss what these objects tell about our society.
  - Give one, Get one: Share and exchange ideas about artefacts from early civilizations.
  - Discuss the "Museum of Innovation."

Big ideas
- Different civilizations throughout time have improved human lives through innovations. (Overall expectation 1)
- Innovations from early civilizations have had an effect on society today. (Overall expectation 2)

Focus questions
- Why do societies need innovations?
- Which innovations from early civilizations help us with daily life today?

Overall expectations

Social Studies	**Language**
- Use a variety of resources and tools to investigate characteristics of a number of early civilizations, including their significant innovations and technological advances. - Show how innovations made by various early civilizations have influenced the modern world.	- Use speaking skills and strategies appropriately to communicate with different audiences for a variety of purposes. - Generate, gather, and organize ideas and information to write for an intended purpose and audience.
The Arts *Visual Arts* - Produce two- and three-dimensional works of art that communicate a range of ideas, thoughts, feelings, and experiences for specific purposes and to specific audiences.	**Mathematics** - Read, represent, compare, and order whole numbers to 100 000, decimal numbers to hundredths, proper and improper fractions, and mixed numbers.

Unit overview	
Specific expectations	**Specific expectations (Modifications)**
Social Studies	
Knowledge and understanding • Identify some scientific and technological advances made by two or more early civilizations (e.g., written language, calendar, time-keeping methods, invention of the wheel, medicine, sculpture, irrigation, building methods, architecture, embalming, aqueducts, metal work).	Benjime: Using a visual representation, such as a timeline or a poster board, show how a scientific or technological advance of an early civilization has changed over time and has eventually influenced modern civilization (e.g., invention of the wheel, sculpture, building methods, architecture, metal work). Min-su and Olesya: Modifications are not necessary. Accommodations outlined in this unit will support their learning.
Inquiry/research and communication skills • Use primary and secondary sources to locate information about early civilizations (e.g., primary sources: artefacts, field trips; secondary sources: atlases, encyclopedias and other print materials, illustrations, videos, CD-ROMs, Internet sites).	Benjime: Use teacher-selected sources/materials to locate information about an early innovation. Min-su and Olesy: Modifications are not necessary. Accommodations outlined in this unit will support their learning.
Application • Make connections between some elements of modern life and similar elements from early civilizations (e.g., the Olympic ideal, democracy, money as a medium of exchange, citizenship, philosophy, mythology, trade, social structures, legal systems, theatre, architecture).	Benjime: Match some elements of modern life to similar elements from an early civilization (e.g., cemetery and pyramid, hieroglyphs and writing, paper and papyrus). Min-su and Olesya: Modifications are not necessary. Accommodations outlined in this unit will support their learning.
• Report on the relevance to modern society of selected scientific and technological discoveries made by early civilizations (e.g., written language, astronomy, irrigation, mathematics, navigational instruments, medicine, architecture, the mining and smelting of metals).	Benjime: Identify some discoveries of early civilizations to show how they are still used today. Min-su and Olesya: Modifications are not necessary. Accommodations outlined in this unit will support their learning.
Language	
Oral communication	
2.3 Communicate orally in a clear, coherent manner, presenting ideas, opinions, and information in a readily understandable form (e.g., present an argument that has a clearly stated purpose, point-by-point development, and relevant supporting details).	2.3 Benjime: Communicate orally using short, rehearsed words and phrases (e.g., make a short presentation about a chosen topic). Min-su and Olesya: Modifications are not necessary. Accommodations outlined in this unit will support their learning.
2.7 Use a variety of appropriate visual aids (e.g., posters, charts, maps, globes, computer-generated organizers) to support or enhance oral presentations (e.g., use ministry-licensed software to create a Venn diagram to compare two different biographies).	2.7 No modification of this expectation is necessary for these ELLs since visual aids are essential for their comprehension of the concepts in this unit. The number and complexity of the visual aids may need to be adjusted for Benjime.
Writing	
1.3 Gather information to support ideas for writing, using a variety of strategies and a range of print and electronic resources (e.g., interview people with knowledge of the topic; identify and use graphic and multimedia sources; keep a record of sources used and information gathered).	1.3 Benjime: With scaffolding, copy words and phrases to record information on a graphic organizer, or glue strips of prepared words and simple phrases in the appropriate places on the graphic organizer. Min-su: Modification is not necessary. He will be supported through scaffolding such as teacher-selected resources that are at an appropriate level and include strong visuals. Olesya: Modifications are not necessary. Accommodations outlined in this unit will support her learning.

Unit overview	
1.6 Determine whether the ideas and information they have gathered are relevant, appropriate, and adequate for the purpose, and do more research if necessary (e.g., review material with a partner using a mind map or timeline).	1.6 Benjime: Because of the complexity of this task, Benjime will be exempted from this expectation. Min-su and Olesya: Modifications are not necessary. Accommodations outlined in this unit will support their learning.
2.8 Produce revised, draft pieces of writing to meet identified criteria based on the expectations related to content, organization, style, and use of conventions.	2.8 Benjime: Because of the complexity of this task, Benjime will be exempted from this expectation. Min-su and Olesya: Modifications are not necessary. Accommodations outlined in this unit will support their learning.

Assessment and evaluation

Assessment for learning	*Assessment for learning*	*Assessment of learning*
• teacher observations	• Self-assessment checklist	• Culminating task rubric

Links to prior knowledge and skills

Students may have first-hand experience or knowledge about one or more of the following: • different societies around the world • the idea that people of different societies may have differing values and beliefs This unit is part of a larger study of early civilizations and students may have already completed activities relating to: • locations of early civilizations • environmental influence • education • family life • social structures • values and beliefs • agriculture	Students may have acquired the following skills before beginning this unit: • using an organizer to collect information • making research notes • generating a rubric • providing and responding to peer feedback • finding and selecting appropriate materials for research • making short presentations in a supported context

Instructional Activities	Modifications / Accommodations for ELLs			Teacher Considerations
	Benjime (Beginner EDL —Stage 1)	Min-su (Intermediate ESL — Stage 2)	Olesya (Advanced ESL — Stages 3 - 4)	

LESSON 1 – INTRODUCTION

Yes/No chart

Instructional Activities	Benjime	Min-su	Olesya	Teacher Considerations
• Demonstrate, using a large T-chart and a series of pictures, how to sort items into the categories "Innovation" and "Non-Innovation." • Students work independently to sort the remaining pictures. • Lead a class discussion to clarify the concept of "innovation." **Assessment for learning** This activity provides information about students' prior knowledge, which will inform planning and instruction.	Benjime may need to work with another student at the beginning of this task. If he demonstrates that he understands this concept, allow him to complete his chart independently.	Work with Min-su for a few minutes to confirm his understanding of both the instructions and concept. Assist him with names of any unfamiliar pictures. He may need to use his bilingual dictionary for some unfamiliar vocabulary.	Include Olesya in the class discussion and help her to extend her use of academic language (e.g., *concept, innovation, invention*).	Use pictures so that all learners can engage easily in the task. Select pictures of common objects that would be familiar to everyone, including recently arrived students. Be sure to make the connection between invention and innovation, and that they may be used interchangeably in this context.

Mystery box

Instructional Activities	Benjime	Min-su	Olesya	Teacher Considerations
• Place three modern objects in a box. • Pull out two objects one at a time and guide the class as they analyze each object (e.g., explain what it is, where it was invented, why it was invented, how the people use it). • Note and post key vocabulary elicited on the word wall. • For the third object, students complete a Think-Pair-Share, generate and share their ideas. • Students illustrate each object and record information beside it.	Benjime works with a partner or the ELD teacher to identify each of the objects and the uses for each. He will record the names and make illustrations of the objects in his word book. He may not be able to participate in the Think-Pair-Share at this point.	Pair Min-su with a supportive partner for the Think-Pair-Share. He will need help with certain words or language structures, especially when recording his ideas on paper.	Monitor Olesya's use of academic language throughout these tasks. Help her to target and use a variety of vocabulary items that are appropriate and effective.	As with any of the tasks in this unit, the instructions must be clear enough for the ELLs to understand. Gestures and visuals will help communicate the goals for the task. Possible objects for the box include a water bottle, a cell phone, and a flashlight. These objects should be familiar to all the students in the room. Benjime will need to work with the teacher to build vocabulary and make connections between items and their uses.

Instructional Activities	Modifications / Accommodations for ELLs			Teacher Considerations
	Benjime (Beginner EDL –Stage 1)	**Min-su** (Intermediate ESL – Stage 2)	**Olesya** (Advanced ESL – Stages 3 - 4)	
Give one, Get one				
• Post a picture of an abacus and pose the questions: "What was this object used for in an early civilization?" and "Who used it?" • Hand out "Give one, Get one" sheet to each student. Students list all possible uses for the abacus. • Students walk around the room to share responses with each other. • They compare and add different ideas to their own list. • Lead follow-up discussion about the abacus's function. Explain how the abacus is related to the modern calculator. • Guide the discussion to how different civilizations developed different counting systems. • Demonstrate how to use the abacus for making simple calculations, such as money transactions.	Benjime works one-on-one with a partner or the ELD teacher to record two or three uses for the abacus. Help him to record his ideas in simple words or pictures. Benjime will practise reading and saying these words before sharing them with his classmates. He will participate in the walk-around phase of this task	Min-su will benefit from a bank of words to use when recording his ideas (e.g., *count, calculate, total, shop keeper, banker, money lender*).	The follow-up discussion will help Olesya confirm her understanding of the words that she used on her sheet and have her put any new vocabulary into her personal dictionary.	An abacus would be helpful to demonstrate to students how it functions. The class is working on "number sense and numeration" using base ten blocks to represent whole numbers. Using the abacus will help the students to make a connection with what they are learning in math. Further connections can be made with Egyptian and Roman counting systems.

Instructional Activities	Modifications / Accommodations for ELLs			Teacher Considerations
	Benjime (Beginner EDL –Stage 1)	**Min-su** (Intermediate ESL – Stage 2)	**Olesya** (Advanced ESL – Stages 3 - 4)	

LESSON 4 – CONDUCT INDIVIDUAL RESEARCH

Instructional Activities	Benjime	Min-su	Olesya	Teacher Considerations
• Students choose one innovation from the group-generated list created during the placemat activity (completed in the preceding lesson). • Provide the students with a research organizer and review how to use it. • Students and teachers establish the criteria for successful performance by collaborating on the production of a rubric for the research task. • Students work individually and with other members of their groups to locate and gather information about their selected innovation. • Design and construct an artefact based on the innovation.	Benjime will be strategically placed with students with whom he is comfortable and familiar. He will use a modified research organizer with a cloze format (5Ws) to record basic details about the innovation. He may require a scribe to help him with some of the words. Benjime will plan with a teacher before designing and constructing his artefact. The teacher will guide Benjime in selecting an appropriate innovation for research. To create his presentation, Benjime will insert the information from the 5W organizer, using sentence starters. He needs multiple opportunities to practise the presentation with classmates or teachers. After practising his presentation with classmates and teachers, Benjime will make it to a small group in the class. He may present to visitors, if he chooses to do so. Use a modified rubric for assessing his success.	Provide Min-su with resources that contain effective visuals. The school library has a collection of materials that are age-appropriate and are intended for use with ELLs. Encourage Min-su to write his parts of his first draft in L1. He will use his bilingual dictionary to help him select appropriate vocabulary for his research notes, and to prepare his presentation notes. Min-su will meet with the classroom teacher or ESL teacher for extra support when editing his writing. Provide him with multiple opportunities to practise the presentation with classmates or teachers.	Review with Olesya the instructions on how to use the organizer. Meet with her during the research phase to check that the materials that she is using are appropriate for her independent reading level and that she understands the information she has recorded. Encourage her to check that she is on track by conferring regularly with other members of her group. Monitor Olesya's work on her organizer to confirm the accuracy of her research notes. Confer with her regularly as she prepares her presentation to ensure correct use of a wide variety of academic and subject-specific terminology.	The students are free to choose any one of many possible innovations for early civilizations, such as tools, buildings, technology, social structures, etc. It is important to help students who choose an abstract concept to select an object that represents that concept (e.g., democracy in Early Greece could be represented by a model of a vote recorded on a broken pot). Benjime and Min-su may be more engaged in the process if they choose an early civilization in or near their country of origin. Rubrics for assessment (even student-generated ones) may be a whole new idea for Benjime and Min-su. They may be silent participants in this task, listening and building the complex concept of rubric and achievement levels. Exposure to the rubric well in advance of the culminating task will ensure that all students, in particular the ELLs, have an opportunity to understand the expectations of this activity. Giving Benjime a 5W organizer to record his research will help him prepare for his presentation. He will use that information to complete sentence starters to create the presentation (e.g., This is a _____; It was used by _____.).

Instructional Activities	Modifications / Accommodations for ELLs			Teacher Considerations
	Benjime (Beginner EDL –Stage 1)	**Min-su** (Intermediate ESL – Stage 2)	**Olesya** (Advanced ESL – Stages 3 - 4)	
CULMINATING TASK				
Museum of Innovations				
• Students set up their exhibits (artefacts and associated research) according to their group plans. • Students display their artefacts in the "Museum of Innovation." • Students make their presentations first to their classmates, and then to a public audience, such as students from other classes and visitors. **Assessment of Learning** • Teacher conducts assessment of student performance, using a teacher-created rubric. **Assessment as learning** • Students use the same checklist to reflect on their own performance and make suggestions for improvement. They respond in writing to the assessment by answering the following questions (added to the bottom of the checklist): • What did you do well in the presentation? • What changes could you make to improve your presentation?	After having practised his short presentation with classmates and teachers, Benjime will make his presentation to a small group in the class. He may also present to visitors, but only if he chooses to do so. Use a modified rubric for assessing his success.	Provide focussed feedback to Min-su including positive comments and suggestions for improvement, such as pronunciation of difficult words and ways to develop fluency.	Olesya has received appropriate support to this point and is ready to make the presentation. In addition to feedback about strengths, it may be necessary, after making the class presentation, to provide Oleysa with focussed feedback on specific linguistic elements (e.g., positive comments, word choice, grammar, sentence structure, nuance of language).	Encourage students to use a variety of presentation formats (e.g., posters, slideshow, diorama, booklet, photomural, interview, news report). Multiple times for practice have been built into this lesson. The students will have many opportunities to make their presentations before others visit the museum. If any student is uncomfortable presenting to an unfamiliar audience, they will not be required to make the presentation and will have been assessed before that time. The students will be aware of the "look-fors" on the checklist because they helped to develop it. ELLs such as Benjime will be assessed using a teacher-made list, because they are working to meet modified expectations.

A step-by-step research process

Materials
- Teacher- and student-selected print, electronic, and visual materials from many sources
- Fact sheets
- Research folders

How it works (10 steps)
1. The teacher guides students in discussing and processing what they see, read, and record while researching a specific topic.
2. Students record what they learn on fact sheets, in short sentences and in their own words.
3. Students regularly meet to share and discuss their knowledge.
4. Once students and the teacher are satisfied that all the facts needed have been recorded on fact sheets, students are ready to put the information into categories.
5. The teacher helps students choose categories for the facts collected. For example, in a project on Ontario, categories might include *Animals*, *History*, *Farming and Food*, or *Winter* Sports, depending on which specific c facts students have collected.
6. For each category, students choose a colour (e.g., all facts about farming and food are coded in green).
7. Students identify a category by placing a coloured dot with each fact (e.g., green dots for the facts on farming and food).
8. Students repeat this process for each category until they have colour-coded all the facts.
9. Next, students cut up all the fact sheets and glue them onto a fresh piece of paper, according to colour.
10. With the facts for a particular category now on one page, students decide how to order, combine, and edit them with peer and teacher support.

The result is a series of related paragraphs, in the students' own words, on a research topic.

Ways for students to use their paragraphs in a presentation:
- Create posters to accompany their research.
- Make an oral presentation (using cue cards, with jot-note prompts) about the poster.
- Prepare quizzes, using formats such as cloze, fill-in-the-blanks, and true/false, to "test" other students following the presentations.

Sample adapted unit framework for Grade 7: Interactions in the environment – Responding to an environmental issue

Ms. Kassum is a Grade 7 classroom teacher with a diverse group of learners that includes three English language learners: Selvam, Ana, and Khalid. She has just finished a unit on ecosystems with her students. She has planned a science and technology unit that will extend her students' awareness from a local to a global focus. She would like them to understand that as true citizens of the world, the choices they make now will affect the future of our planet. She collaboratively planned with the other Grade 7 classroom teachers. She also made connections with the teacher-librarian and computer support teacher.

The following unit plan includes opportunities for making cross-curricular connections, meeting a range of expectations, and addressing different learning styles. It builds on previously developed skills, such as what the students have learned about online research, as a springboard for new learning. This unit provides opportunities to make connections with the prior knowledge and experience of all the learners in the classroom. When planning, she is careful to consider the needs of all students, including the following ELLs.

ESL	ESD	ESL
Selvam, Beginner early Stage 2 of Second Language Acquisition	**Ana, Intermediate** Stage 2 ELD of Second Language Acquisition	**Khalid, Advanced** Stages 3 – 4 of Second Language Acquisition
Selvam and his mother have been in Canada for just over one year. He had studied some English at school in his country of origin, although the instruction focussed more on independent reading and writing skills than on oral communication. As a result, Selvam is most comfortable when tasks require that he respond in writing. He frequently uses his bilingual dictionary to confirm the spelling and meaning of new words. He likes reading graphic novels and often chooses that format when writing his own stories because it allows him to use his artistic skills. Selvam is beginning to gain confidence when speaking in front of the whole class. He excels in math and he understands the concepts well but finds the language in math challenging. He is learning to play guitar and has performed for his class on several occasions.	Ana arrived in Canada when she was four years old. Since then, Ana's family has migrated between Canada and her home country almost every year. Some of these trips have been as long as six months, during which she did not receive formal schooling. As a result, she does not have age appropriate literacy skills in her home language. She is now in a Grade 7 classroom and may have an extended absence this winter. While in Canada, Ana attends school regularly. She makes good progress with the targeted support of her classroom teacher and the ESL/ELD teacher. Ana enjoys participating orally in many classroom activities, especially those with which she has had personal experience. She enjoys watching movies and listening to her teacher read aloud. She can read and understand simple stories and texts, and often visits the school library to select short chapter books that feature girls her own age. Ana maintains a personal word book and is beginning to use the class word charts more frequently. Her hobbies include keeping a sketchbook and playing basketball.	In the five years prior to his arrival in Canada, Khalid lived in three countries, where he attended school full time and began to develop literacy skills in the languages of instruction. His parents have helped him to maintain and develop literacy in L1 by reading with him at home and enrolling him in an International Languages program. As a result, Khalid is able to read and write at an age-appropriate level in L1. This has given him a strong foundation on which to build his English-language skills. He loves soccer and field hockey and was a member of the teams in some of his former schools. He has now been in Canada for two years and is able to participate in most social conversations, especially those about sports. Khalid sometimes demonstrates leadership in group activities that involve drama or team work. He has just become a member of the school Ambassadors Club which helps welcome newcomer students and their families to their school. He is beginning to understand, appreciate, and use humour with friends.

Unit overview			
Title	*Responding to an environmental concern*	**Grade(s)**	7

Summary of unit

Students research and examine an environmental issue. They prepare and present their findings in a student-led community summit on the environment for the school community (students, parents, teachers, leaders, and other community members). (This unit is adapted from a unit included in *The Ontario Curriculum – Exemplars, Grades 7 and 8 Science & Technology, 2002*).

Scope and sequence

The following list outlines all components of the unit. Three components (marked ★) are later presented in detail to illustrate planning to differentiate instruction for English language learners: (Note that lessons will be of varying lengths, and individual lessons may be carried out over a period of several days.)

Planning with the end in mind

- ■ **Culminating task – Take part in the environmental summit ★**
  - • Present, in chosen format, the results of research that explores an environmental issue, considers differing points of view and responses, and analyzes the implications for the future of the planet.
  - • View and participate in the presentations of other students.

- ■ **Lesson 4 – Plan the presentation**
  - • Observe teacher think-aloud of planning for the presentation.
  - • Make decisions about how to present the information.
  - • Participate in consultations throughout the planning process.
  - • Create, edit, and rehearse (multiple times) the presentation.

- ■ **Lesson 3 – Conduct the research**
  - • Observe teacher modelling of the research process.
  - • Choose a topic that is personally relevant and/or motivating.
  - • Locate and gather information.
  - • Make research notes, using a variety of formats, including graphic organizers.
  - • Participate in consultations (teacher-student, student-student) throughout the research process. ★
  - • Analyze each other's strategies for protecting the environment.

- ■ **Lesson 2 – Visit a local ravine or outdoor education facility**
  - • Observe environmental features which indicate changes that have occurred, and identify possible reasons for these changes

- ■ **Lesson 1 – Introductory lesson**
  - • Participate in tasks to activate prior knowledge: Graffiti Wall and Gallery Walk ★

Big ideas

- • Ecosystems are in a constant state of change. The changes may be caused by nature or by human intervention. (Overall expectations 1 and 2)
- • Human activities have the potential to alter the environment. Humans must be aware of these impacts and try to control them. (Overall expectation 1)

Focus questions

- • How do you feel about the way that we are treating our planet's environment?
- • What would you like to say to others about how we should take care of the Earth?

Unit overview	
Overall expectations	
Language *Reading* • Read and demonstrate an understanding of a variety of literary, graphic, and informational texts, using a range of strategies to construct meaning. *Writing* • Generate, gather, and organize ideas and information to write for an intended purpose and audience. • Draft and revise their writing, using a variety of informational, literary, and graphic forms and stylistic elements appropriate for the purpose and audience. • Use editing, proofreading, and publishing skills and strategies, and knowledge of language conventions to correct errors, refine expression, and present their work effectively. *Media literacy* • Create a variety of media texts for different purposes and audiences, using appropriate forms, conventions and techniques.	**Science and Technology** • Assess the impacts of human activities and technologies on the environment, and evaluate ways of controlling these impacts. • Investigate interactions within the environment, and identify factors that affect the balance between different components of an ecosystem. **Geography** *Natural resources* • Describe positive and negative ways in which human activity can affect resource sustainability and the health of the environment. **Mathematics** • Data management and probability • Make and evaluate convincing arguments based on the analysis of data.
Specific expectations	**Specific expectations (Modifications)**
Science and Technology	
Relating science and technology to society and the environment 1.2 Analyze the costs and benefits of selected strategies for protecting the environment.	1.2 Selvam: Identify the costs and benefits for one strategy for protecting the environment (e.g., methods of reducing carbon emissions of different modes of transportation), using a graphic organizer. Ana and Khalid: Modifications are not necessary. Accommodations outlined in this unit will support their learning.
Developing investigation and communication skills 2.3 Use scientific inquiry/research skills to investigate occurrences (e.g., a forest fire, a drought, an infestation of invasive species such as zebra mussels in a local lake or purple loosestrife in a wetland habitat) that affect the balance within a local ecosystem.	2.3 Modifications are not necessary for ELLs. Accommodations outlined in this unit will support their learning.
2.4 Use appropriate science and technology vocabulary, including *sustainability, biotic, ecosystem, community, population*, and *producer*, in oral and written communication.	2.4 Modifications are not necessary for ELLs. Accommodations outlined in this unit will support their learning.
2.5 Use a variety of forms (e.g., oral, written, graphic, multimedia) to communicate with different audiences and for a variety of purposes (e.g., design a multimedia presentation explaining the interrelationships between biotic and abiotic components in a specific ecosystem).	2.5 Modifications are not necessary for ELLs. Accommodations outlined in this unit will support their learning.

Unit overview	
Language	
Reading	
1.4 Demonstrate understanding of increasingly complex texts by summarizing important ideas and citing a variety of details that support the main idea (e.g., key information in manuals, surveys, graphs, online and print encyclopedias, websites, tables and charts, theme and related ideas in magazine articles, dramatic monologues, television programs).	1.4 Modification for beginner level ELLs (Stages of Second-Language Acquisition – Stage 1): Demonstrate understanding of simple texts by summarizing important ideas and citing two details that support the main idea (with some teacher support). ELLs will require the accommodation of the provision of selected multi-level resources that reflect the independent reading level, the cultural background, and prior learning of individual students.
Writing	
1.3 Gather information to support ideas for writing, using a variety of strategies and a wide range of print and electronic resources (e.g., use a timeline to organize research tasks, interview people with knowledge of the topic, identify and use appropriate graphic and multimedia resources, record sources used and information gathered in a form that makes it easy to understand and retrieve).	1.3 Modifications are not necessary for ELLs. Accommodations outlined in this unit will support their learning.
Media literacy	
3.4 Produce a variety of media texts of some technical complexity for specific purposes and audiences, using appropriate forms, conventions, and techniques.	3.4 Modification for beginner ELLs (Stages of Second-language Acquisition – Stage 1): Produce a simple media text of some technical complexity for specific purposes, using appropriate forms, conventions, and techniques.
4.1 Identify what strategies they found most helpful in making sense of and creating media texts, and explain how these and other strategies can help them improve as media viewers/listeners/producers.	4.1 Accommodations outlined in this unit will support ELL learning.

Assessment and evaluation

Assessment for learning	*Assessment as learning*	*Assessment of learning*
• teacher observation during student performance of graffiti wall and gallery walk activity • student-teacher conferences throughout research process	• student self-and peer-reflection (reflection journal entries)	• rubric to assess culminating task generated by teacher and students • ESL modified rubric developed by the teacher based on the class-developed rubric

Links to prior knowledge and skills

Students may have first-hand experience or knowledge about one or more of the following: • water (e.g., pollution, disease, treatment, public access, sustainability, bottled water, electricity) • air (e.g., pollution, disease, impacts on health) • land (e.g., agriculture, pesticide use, ownership, responsible land use, mining and forestry) • refuse (e.g., management, landfills, recycling, packaging) • technology (e.g., cell phones, microwaves, batteries) • global issues (e.g., global warming, ozone and carbon dioxide, UV index) • community response to environmental issues (e.g., Earth Day initiatives, recycling programs, composting)	Students may have acquired the following skills before beginning this unit: • research skills • sources of information (locating sources, evaluating bias) • consolidating information from a variety of sources • understanding text features • summarizing • making inferences • making connections • organizing information • asking and answering questions Students will have participated in a variety of journal writing activities in advance of the unit. Some students may require explicit instruction or reminders about the protocols of responding to the work of others.

Instructional Activities	Modifications / Accommodations for ELLs			Teacher Considerations
	Selvam Beginner ESL – Stage 2 of Second-Language Acquisition	**Ana** Intermediate ELD – Stage 2 of Second-Language Acquisition	**Khalid** Advanced ESL - Stages 3-4 of Second-Language Acquisition	

LESSON 1 – INTRODUCTORY LESSON

Graffiti Wall and Gallery Walk

Instructional Activities	Selvam	Ana	Khalid	Teacher Considerations
• Post around the room many pictures of environmental issues/disasters from places around the world. • Students examine each picture and record with a single word, phrase, or sketch their observations, thoughts, and reactions on chart paper.	Selvam can respond using familiar words or phrases, using his bilingual dictionary, his first language, or drawings or sketches.	Ana can choose to respond with drawings or sketches as well as words or phrases.	Khalid will not require further differentiation to complete this task.	Choose a wide range of pictures representing environmental concerns from around the globe to ensure that there are issues students are familiar with as well as issues that students may not yet be aware of. Although most learners in the classroom are able to record fully detailed responses to these pictures, a few may not, including Ana. Allowing the students to respond in pictures as well as words or phrases will give her an opportunity to fully participate in this activity. This also takes into account the learning styles of the other students in the room.
• Distribute three stickers of different colours to each student. In a gallery walk, students read others' responses. • They place a sticker of one colour beside one response they strongly agree with, a sticker of another colour beside one response that surprised them, and a third sticker beside one response that they would like to know more about.	Selvam can use his bilingual dictionary, as needed.	Ana will work with a supportive partner here so that she is able to access all of the responses.	Check during the class discussion to ensure that Khalid has fully grasped the academic language of the graffiti wall.	This task will establish a starting point for both the students and the teacher. It will help identify gaps and raise awareness of both local and global issues and resources. Consider ways to capitalize on student interests and personal experience to lead them in their discovery and learning.
• Lead the class in a discussion to analyze trends and patterns in the student responses and the implications for the upcoming research and presentation at the summit (e.g., students may be disturbed by a picture which demonstrates the effects of an oil spill on local wildlife). • Add new terms to the unit word chart as they are identified.				

Instructional Activities	Modifications / Accommodations for ELLs			Teacher Considerations
	Selvam Beginner ESL – Stage 2 of Second-Language Acquisition	**Ana** Intermediate ELD – Stage 2 of Second-Language Acquisition	**Khalid** Advanced ESL - Stages 3-4 of Second-Language Acquisition	
Assessment as learning				
Students complete a guided reflective journal entry. Students write paragraphs using each of the following starters: • *I agreed with _____ because…* • *I was surprised by ____ because…* • *I want to know more about _____ because…*	Remind Selvam to access the vocabulary of the unit word chart.	For Ana, the emphasis will be on the expression of her thoughts, rather than the accuracy of her spelling and grammar.	Encourage Khalid to provide greater depth of response and to extend his use of academic vocabulary by asking him to plan his responses using a word web.	Ana may need more time than the others to fully organize her thoughts. Give her the opportunity to express her ideas.
• Distribute envelopes containing smaller versions of the posted pictures to pairs or triads. • Students work together to group pictures and generate category titles (e.g., human-created/natural; local/national/international/global; water/air/land/refuse/technology). • Lead a whole-class discussion to synthesize category titles.	Provide Selvam's group with a few prompts useful for completing this task (e.g., "I think this picture goes with this one because…").	Within her group, pair Ana with another student who will model categorization for her.	Khalid will not require further differentiation to complete this task.	If available, use the white board so the class can manipulate and edit the images and category titles when working as a large group. Selvam and Ana need to be paired with supportive peers.
• Students look for songs with lyrics about the effect of human behaviours on the environment. • Distribute a cloze activity with the lyrics of one song for students to complete. • Discuss the meanings of the words and the overall message of the song. Identify the literary elements (e.g., metaphor) in the song.	Give Selvam a modified cloze in which the teacher provides a word bank that contains more words than blanks in the text.	Provide Ana with the lyrics and media file of the song prior to this lesson. A parent volunteer could work with Ana to help her preview and begin to understand this song.	Give Khalid a modified cloze with a word bank that has only the most challenging words. He will complete much of the task independently.	Students might choose songs in other languages, to bring a more global perspective to the activity. Supplement the students' selections of songs, as necessary.
• Students reflect on their personal reaction to the song through interactive writing.	Help Selvam and Ana to organize their ideas by reviewing adjectives that describe feelings and appropriate ways to express opinions and advice.		After Khalid has written his response, invite him to join other students who are also working on revision skills.	Preview with Ana and Selvam the vocabulary and language structures they need prior to this lesson. Many students in the class need the visual references of anchor charts that outline the writing process.

Instructional Activities	Modifications / Accommodations for ELLs			Teacher Considerations
	Selvam Beginner ESL – Stage 2 of Second-Language Acquisition	**Ana** Intermediate ELD – Stage 2 of Second-Language Acquisition	**Khalid** Advanced ESL - Stages 3-4 of Second-Language Acquisition	
• Teacher provides focus questions: – How do you feel about the way that we are treating our planet's environment? – What would you like to say to others about how we should take care of our world?	Provide Selvam with an opportunity to rehearse his response orally before he begins to write.	Ana can consult a learner dictionary and her personal word book to complete sentence starters. Because she will need more time, she will complete her journal in the homework club.		The ESL/ELD teacher has suggested strategic use of first language as a strategy to help some students commit their ideas more easily to paper.
• Students read and respond to another student's journal entry. Provide the sentence starter: *I agree/disagree with _____'s ideas because…*	Selvam will use his personal dictionary to reference phrases to respond to the journal entry.	Ana will work collaboratively with a classmate who will read aloud his or her journal entry and Ana will respond orally.	Khalid will refer to a modelled response to ensure that he has fully and correctly explained his ideas in his entry.	Some students may feel more comfortable sharing their response with the teacher instead of the large group.

LESSON 2 – CONDUCT THE RESEARCH

Participate in consultations

• Select one environmental issue and model for the class the research process. • Students conduct research independently or with a partner. • Conduct individual conferences with students throughout the research process. • As a whole class activity, share with students the learning expectations addressed in the culminating task. • Help students deconstruct the expectations to describe learning behaviours at all four levels of achievement. Accompanying the rubric, include opportunities for student self-reflection and goal setting. • Create the rubric with the students. • Create a modified rubric for/ with beginner ELLs (Stage 1 of Second-Language Acquisition). **Assessment for learning** Students will engage in self-assessment, using the rubric.	Selvam will participate in this process using carefully chosen resources that include visuals, a glossary, and clearly presented information. He may use a bilingual dictionary. Frequent conferencing ensures that he is clear about the task.	Ana will partner with a peer who chose the same environmental issue. Frequent student-teacher consultations will keep them on task and ensure that Ana fully engages in all parts of the process.	The scheduled conferences will help Khalid edit and review his written work. It will be important to help him extend his use of complex sentence structures and vocabulary (e.g., *summarize, pollution, advocacy*).	Students educated outside of Ontario may have had different experiences and instruction around research. Post a chart of the research process and vocabulary for students to reference. Continue to add to the class word chart new vocabulary that students encounter in their research. Exposure to the rubric well in advance of the culminating task will ensure that all students, in particular ELLs, have ample opportunity to understand the expectations of the activity.

Instructional Activities	Modifications / Accommodations for ELLs			Teacher Considerations
	Selvam Beginner ESL – Stage 2 of Second-Language Acquisition	**Ana** Intermediate ELD – Stage 2 of Second-Language Acquisition	**Khalid** Advanced ESL - Stages 3–4 of Second-Language Acquisition	
CULMINATING TASK				
Take part in the environmental summit				
• Conduct a whole-class discussion on personal strengths and preferences as they relate to presentation formats. • Students select a format for their summit presentation. • Students participate in the environmental summit. **Assessment as learning** Students refer to the rubric to set goals for high achievement. They rehearse their presentations for a variety of audiences. **Assessment of Learning** Teacher uses the class-created rubric to evaluate student achievement of the overall expectations.	Selvam wrote and recorded a song about litter and the lack of recycling efforts in the school. He took pictures around the school community and created an electronic presentation. At the summit, he performed the song to accompany the presentation and invited participants to join in.	In front of a small group and in advance of the summit, the teacher videotaped Ana's presentation on the destruction of the rain forest in her homeland. Ana drew a series of posters to show what the rainforest looked like many years ago, how it is being depleted, and predicted what it would look like in the future if current practices continue. She used posters as graphic organizers to demonstrate her learning. At the summit, Ana introduced the video by reading a script she had prepared in advance.	Khalid introduced his presentation by highlighting, using charts and graphs, the amount of bottled water his soccer team consumed over the past six months. Khalid wrote a script and presented a dramatic monologue related to the issues surrounding bottled water.	*Post-summit reflection* It is important to create an opportunity for each student to select a personally relevant topic and presentation format. Planning with students' readiness, learning styles, and interests in mind contributed to success for all. Selvam's decision to use music helped him to stay engaged throughout the research process. Because of Ana's anxiety when reading in front of a large group, she pre-taped her presentation in front of a small familiar group. Khalid's love of soccer engaged him so he reached deeper into both content and language. Collect samples of student work for use as exemplars with future groups.

Glossary

The following definitions, including examples, are intended to help teachers and parents use this document. It should be noted that the examples provided are suggestions and are not meant to be exhaustive.

authentic language task A language learning task that involves using language to communicate a message and/or accomplish a purpose in a real-world situation.

basic interpersonal communication skills (BICS) Face-to-face language skills used in everyday communication – listening, speaking, carrying on basic conversations, and getting one's basic needs met. Typically, English language learners acquire basic interpersonal communication skills before they develop proficiency in more complex, academic language.

cognitive academic language proficiency (CALP) Language proficiency associated with schooling and the abstract language abilities required for academic work. A more complex, conceptual, linguistic ability than conversational language, CALP includes facility in analysis, synthesis, and evaluation. English language learners need at least five years to develop cognitive academic language proficiency in English.

comprehensible input Language that is made comprehensible to the learner through the use of visual aids, familiar content, rephrasing, repetition, and other means.

content-based language instruction An instructional approach in which topics related to curriculum content are used as the vehicle for second-language learning. These topics are often delivered through thematic units. Students thus acquire important curriculum-based knowledge and skills at the same time as they learn language.

conventions Accepted practices or rules in the use of language. In written or printed materials, some conventions help convey meaning (e.g., punctuation, typeface, capital letters) and other conventions aid in the presentation of content (e.g., table of contents, headings, footnotes, charts, captions, lists, pictures, index). See also **text features**.

ELL English language learner.

errors and mistakes The result of English language learners' incomplete knowledge of the language as they attempt to reproduce the patterns they hear and read. Making *errors* is a normal and necessary part of language learning; errors disappear as knowledge of the language becomes more complete, while others appear as learners begin to experiment with more complex forms of the language. Students may slip occasionally and make a *mistake* with something they have previously learned, especially in stressful situations.

first language The language a child first learned as an infant. See also **home language.**

high frequency/low frequency vocabulary Certain aspects of language, such as individual words, that can be counted in terms of how often they occur in the oral and written language environment. English language learners acquire the most frequently occurring words first, because they encounter these words so often in natural language contexts. Low-frequency words occur less often in daily life but are required for success in school. Most English language learners will require specific instruction and practice in order to learn these words.

home language The language spoken at home between family members. Generally, this is the first language that children learn.

pronunciation and accent English language learners in the primary and junior grades acquire the sound system of English by imitating the language they hear around them. If they have frequent opportunities for communication with speakers of Standard Canadian English (e.g., through structured group activities in the classroom), they will probably acquire a local accent very quickly. However, older students may find some aspects of English pronunciation more difficult. This is partly because by this age, the sound system of their own language is so firmly established that attempting to produce sounds or patterns of sound that do not exist in their own language feels unnatural. Students may require direct instruction to learn some aspects of pronunciation (e.g., the distinction between the sounds represented in print by *v* and *b*).

register A style of language (e.g., formal, colloquial) appropriate to a specific audience, purpose, or situation. Register is determined by the level of formality in a particular social setting, the relationship among the individuals involved in the communication, and the purpose of the interaction.

scaffolding The provision of sufficient supports (e.g., learning strategies, guidance, resources) to promote learning. The "scaffolds" selected by the teacher are intended to help the student move to higher levels of achievement and transfer the responsibility for learning from the teacher to the student, thereby fostering independence. Scaffolding proceeds by determining the student's zone of proximal development and designing adjustable support and guidance.

scribing Writing down verbatim the words dictated by a student.

sentence patterns The characteristic grammatical structures or patterns of English that influence such things as word order and the use of prefixes, suffixes, prepositions, articles, and auxiliary verbs (e.g., to form questions and negatives: "Do you speak English?"; "I don't eat hot dogs.").

sentence starters The first few words of a sentence that the teacher provides students to help them structure their written or oral response and which allow students to use constructions that are slightly more complex than their current proficiency level.

syntax The predictable structure of a language and the ways in which words are combined to form phrases, clauses, and sentences. Syntax includes classes of words (e.g., nouns, verbs, adjectives) and their functions (e.g., subject, object).

transition words and phrases Words and phrases that link and/or signal relationships between clauses, sentences, or paragraphs. For example, *after* and *before* show relationships with respect to time; *in comparison* and *however* show relationships of similarity and difference.

varieties of English English is an international language and many varieties of English - sometimes referred to as dialects – are spoken around the world. Standard English is the variety of English that is used as the language of education, law, and government in English-speaking countries. Some varieties of English are very different – not only in pronunciation or accent but also in vocabulary and sentence structure – from the English required for success in Ontario schools. Some varieties are so different from standard English that many linguists consider them to be languages in their own right.

Resources

Association for Supervision and Curriculum Development. (December 2004/January 2005). Educating Language Learners. *Educational Leadership, 62* (4).

> This resource is a special issue of the journal *Educational Leadership* that examines the issues surrounding English language learning in schools from a number of different perspectives.

Carrasquillo, A.L., Kucer, S., & Abrams, R. (2004). *Beyond the beginnings: Literacy interventions for upper elementary English language learners.* Clevedon, UK: Multilingual Matters.

> The authors offer detailed suggestions on literacy practices for English language learners who have acquired everyday language fluency and basic literacy skills in English, but still need support in developing academic language skills.

Cary, S. (2007). *Working with English language learners: Answers to teachers' top ten questions.* Portsmouth, NH: Heinemann.

> This book provides clear, practical advice to teachers who are new to working with English language learners. Using classroom scenarios, Cary poses and answers common teacher questions such as, "How do I make my spoken language more understandable?", "How can I make a difficult textbook more readable?", and "How can I teach grade level content to beginners?".

Coelho, E. (2007). *Adding English: A guide to teaching in multilingual classrooms.* Toronto, ON: Pippin Publishing.

> Comprehensive and clear, with a distinct Canadian focus, this is an excellent resource book for understanding and working with English language learners that can be referred to for a wide variety of information and suggestions.

Coggins, D., Kravin, D., Coates, G.D., & Carroll, M.D. (2007). *English language learners in the mathematics classroom.* Thousand Oaks, CA: Corwin Press.

> Written by four mathematics teaching experts, this book offers guidelines and strategies, illustrated with classroom vignettes, on how to make the learning of mathematics less language-dependent, while at the same time working with English language learners on their development of English for mathematics.

Cummins, J., Brown, K., & Sayers, D. (2007). *Literacy, technology, and diversity: Teaching for success in changing times.* Boston, MA: Allyn & Bacon.

> This book Includes guidelines for the appropriate use of technology that also develops higher-order thinking skills and academic language proficiency. It contains interesting case studies in classroom and community projects that involve and engage ELLs, particularly those from low socio-economic backgrounds.

Dragan, P. B. (2005). *A how-to guide for teaching English language learners in the primary classroom.* Portsmouth, NH: Heinemann.

> Written by a classroom teacher who obviously enjoys teaching and learning from her English language learners, this book offers suggestions – rooted largely in the use of literature, drama, and music – for connecting with primary-aged children who are beginning to learn English.

Freeman, D., & Freeman, Y. (2007). *English language learners: The essential guide.* New York, NY: Scholastic.

> This book provides suggestions for classroom teachers as to how to support language growth through content areas, organize curriculum around themes, draw on English language learners' first languages and cultures, emphasize meaningful reading and writing, and develop academic language.

Gibbons, P. (2002). *Scaffolding language, scaffolding learning: Teaching second language learners in the mainstream classroom.* Portsmouth, NH: Heinemann.

> This book explains why scaffolding is important for English language learners and provides practical advice for K - 8 classroom teachers on using scaffolding techniques.

Hamayan, E., and Freeman, R. (Eds.). (2006). *English language learners at school: A guide for administrators.* Philadelphia, PA: Caslon Publishing.

> This resource provides articulate expertise and advice on a range of topics for administrators who lead schools with both large and small populations of English language learners.

Hamayan, E., Marler, B., Sanchez-Lopez, C., & Damico, J. (2007). *Special education considerations for English language learners: Delivering a continuum of services.* Philadelphia, PA: Caslon Publishing.

> This resource outlines a comprehensive approach, including assessment and intervention suggestions, to the challenging task of teasing apart the factors at play in the decision as to whether an English language learner who is experiencing some difficulty in learning the new language may need referral for further psycho-educational testing and support.

Houk, F.A. (2005). *Supporting English language learners: A guide for teachers and administrators.* Portsmouth, NH: Heinemann.

> Written by an experienced elementary school teacher, this book combines background discussion of the broad themes behind successful programs for English language learners with practical ideas on to how to teach and advocate for these students.

Rothenberg, C., & Fisher, D. (2007). *Teaching English language learners: A differentiated approach.* New Jersey, NJ: Pearson Education.

> This resource offers well-grounded advice on designing high-expectation instruction that considers the individual needs of English language learners and ensures that building on learners' prior knowledge is placed at the forefront in teaching.

Samway, K.D., & McKeon, D. (2007). *Myths and realities: Best practices for English language learners.* Portsmouth, NH: Heinemann.

> This book dismantles commonly believed myths about English language learners and provides a description of what really helps them to learn both their new language and to succeed in school.

Schecter, S.R., & Cummins, J. (2003). *Multilingual education in practice: Using diversity as a resource.* Portsmouth, NH: Heinemann.

> This resource offers a framework for developing an inclusive and effective curriculum for English language learners. The focus is on new arrivals, how to build on the language and cultural knowledge that students bring with them, and the kind of administrative leadership that is key to establishing a welcoming and open climate in schools within which English language learners will flourish.

Ontario Ministry of Education Resources

Aménagement linguistique – A Policy for Ontario's French-Language Schools and Francophone Community, 2004.

Early Reading Strategy: The Report of the Expert Panel on Early Reading in Ontario, 2003.

Education for All: The Report of the Expert Panel on Literacy and Numeracy Instruction for Students with Special Education Needs, Kindergarten to Grade 6, 2005.

English Language Learners/ESL and ELD Programs and Services: Policies and Procedures for Ontario Elementary and Secondary Schools, Kindergarten to Grade 12, 2007.

Finding Common Ground: Character Development in Ontario Schools, K - 12, June 2008.

A Guide to Effective Instruction in Mathematics, Kindergarten to Grade 6: Volume One – Foundations of Mathematics Instruction, 2006.

A Guide to Effective Instruction in Mathematics, Kindergarten to Grade 6: Volume Two – Problem Solving and Communication, 2006.

A Guide to Effective Instruction in Mathematics, Kindergarten to Grade 6: Volume Three – Classroom Resources and Management, 2006.

A Guide to Effective Instruction in Mathematics, Kindergarten to Grade 6: Volume Four – Assessment and Home Connections, 2006.

A Guide to Effective Instruction in Mathematics, Kindergarten to Grade 6: Volume Five – Teaching Basic Facts and Multidigit Computations, 2006.

A Guide to Effective Instruction in Reading: Kindergarten to Grade 3, 2003.

A Guide to Effective Instruction in Writing: Kindergarten to Grade 3, 2003.

A Guide to Effective Literacy Instruction, Grades 4 to 6: Volume One – Foundations of Literacy Instruction for the Junior Learner, 2006.

A Guide to Effective Literacy Instruction, Grades 4 to 6: Volume Two – Assessment, 2006.

A Guide to Effective Literacy Instruction, Grades 4 to 6: Volume Three - Planning and Classroom Management, 2006.

A Guide to Effective Literacy Instruction, Grades 4 to 6: Volume Four – Oral Language, 2008.

A Guide to Effective Literacy Instruction, Grades 4 to 6: Volume Five – Reading, 2008.

A Guide to Effective Literacy Instruction, Grades 4 to 6: Volume Six – Writing, 2008.

A Guide to Effective Literacy Instruction, Grades 4 to 6: Volume Seven – Media Literacy, 2008.

Helping Your Child Do Mathematics: A Guide for Parents, Kindergarten to Grade 6, 2007. (Available in multiple languages)

Helping Your Child with Reading and Writing: A Guide for Parents, Kindergarten to Grade 6, 2007. (Available in multiple languages)

Literacy for Learning: The Report of the Expert Panel on Literacy in Grades 4 to 6 in Ontario, 2004.

Many Roots, Many Voices: Supporting English Language Learners in Every Classroom. A Practical Guide for Ontario Educators, 2005.

The Ontario Curriculum, Grades 9-12: English as a Second Language and English Literacy Development, Revised, 2007.

The Ontario Curriculum Grades 1-8: Language, 2006.

Reach Every Student – Energizing Ontario Education, 2008.

Supporting English Language Learners in Kindergarten: A Practical Guide for Ontario Educators, 2007.

Supporting English Language Learners with Limited Prior Schooling: A Practical Guide for Ontario Educators, Grades 3 to 12, 2008.

Teaching and Learning Mathematics: The Report of the Expert Panel on Mathematics in Grades 4 to 6 in Ontario, 2004.

TIPS for English Language Learners in Mathematics, Grades 7, 8, 9 Applied, 10 Applied, 2005.

Appendix

Descriptions of Skills at the Four Stages of Second-Language Acquisition and Literacy Development

A. Stages of Second-Language Acquisition and Literacy Development for ESL Students

B. Stages of Second-Language Acquisition and Literacy Development for ELD Students

*The Ontario Curriculum, Grades 1 – 8: English As a Second Language and
English Literacy Development – A Resource Guide, 2001.*

Table A1.1: ESL, Grades 1 to 3 – Listening

Stage 1 Students understand basic spoken English. They:	**Stage 2** Students understand key information presented in highly supported contexts in a variety of settings. They:	**Stage 3** Students understand social English, but They: require contextual support to understand academic language. They:	**Stage 4** Students understand spoken English in most contexts. They:
– follow simple directions with support from visual cues – respond to clear, short, simple questions – respond briefly to short, simple stories, songs, and poems – respond to familiar conversational topics using single words and short phrases – respond to gestures, courtesies, and tones of voice, and follow classroom routines	– participate in conversations on familiar topics – understand key vocabulary and concepts related to a theme/topic – request clarification when necessary – respond to direct questions, frequently used commands, courtesies, and some humour – respond to non-verbal signals in familiar contexts – begin to respond to unseen speakers (e.g., on the radio, on the telephone, over the school public-address system) – identify main ideas in visually supported oral presentations containing familiar vocabulary	– respond to discussions and conversations – identify key information in most contexts, with the aid of some repetition – respond appropriately to body language, non-verbal signals, tone of voice, pauses, stress, and intonation – respond to unseen speakers (e.g., over the school public-address system, on the radio, on the telephone) – follow a series of simple instructions	– participate in most social and academic discussions – respond to complex sentences – understand age-appropriate expressions and idioms

Table A1.2: ESL, Grades 1 to 3 – Speaking

Stage 1 Students speak English for basic communication. They:	**Stage 2** Students speak English with increasing spontaneity and accuracy. They:	**Stage 3** Students initiate conversations and participate in discussions and presentations using a variety of strategies. They:	**Stage 4** Students speak English accurately in most situations. They:
– use short, patterned questions to seek information – share personal information (e.g., name, address) – express basic needs using single words – identify familiar names, objects, and actions – speak with sufficient clarity for teacher comprehension – begin to use (with assistance) subject–predicate order, simple verb tenses, negatives, questions, plurals, pronouns, adjectives, adverbs, common contractions, and basic prepositions of location and direction – imitate some English stress and intonation patterns – use everyday gestures and courtesies to convey meaning – participate in short, prepared role plays and dialogues	– ask simple questions – participate in social discussions using short phrases and short sentences – participate, with prompting, in academic discussions, using short phrases and short sentences – initiate and maintain face-to-face conversations – recount familiar events, stories, and key information – give simple directions or instructions and communicate simple observations – express personal opinions and emotions – speak with sufficient clarity and accuracy for listener comprehension – speak at almost the pace of first-language speakers, showing some control of stress, timing, and rhythm – express meaning with growing competence, using present and past verb tenses when explaining causes and results, direction, and time	– initiate and maintain conversations – participate in discussions based on classroom themes – make short, effective oral presentations in an academic context – speak with clear pronunciation and enunciation – begin to self-correct simple grammatical errors – use voice to indicate emphasis through pacing, volume, intonation, and stress	– use most language structures appropriate to the grade level – speak with fluency and clarity in group situations – self-correct common grammatical errors – make academic presentations – use idiomatic and colloquial language appropriately

Table A1.3: ESL, Grades 1 to 3 – Reading

Stage 1 Students read and comprehend simple written English. They:	Stage 2 Students read for specific purposes when background knowledge and vocabulary are familiar. They:	Stage 3 Students demonstrate increasing independence in a variety of reading tasks, with ongoing support. They:	Stage 4 Students demonstrate control of grade-appropriate reading tasks. They:
– recognize the alphabet in print – know the direction of English print – read pictures and use picture clues – begin to use phonetic and context clues and sight recognition to understand simple texts (e.g., pattern books, chart stories, songs, chants, rhymes) – recognize familiar words and repeated phrases in plays, poems, stories, and environmental print – participate in shared reading activities, choral reading, and rehearsed reading in a small group – select appropriate reading materials, with assistance	– use reading strategies to assist in deriving meaning from text (e.g., predicting; rereading; phonics; recognition of cueing systems, repetition, and word families) – understand familiar vocabulary in age-appropriate stories, poems, scripts, environmental print, and computer text – select main ideas in short, familiar passages from a variety of genres – use some correct phrasing and rhythm when reading familiar material aloud – use the school library, with assistance, to find personal reading materials for enjoyment and information	– begin to follow written instructions – describe story components (e.g., character, plot, setting) – read and understand grade-appropriate text, with minimal assistance – use grade-appropriate resources that provide some visual or contextual support (e.g., graphic organizers, class word lists, theme-book collections, environmental print, picture dictionary, table of contents)	– respond independently to written instructions – recall and retell a written story – figure out meaning in text that may be unfamiliar, unsupported by visual context, and contain challenging vocabulary and sentence structures – read a variety of print material – begin to use independent research skills in the classroom and school library – choose and enjoy material for personal reading similar in scope and difficulty to that being read by peers

Table A1.4: ESL, Grades 1 to 3 – Writing

Stage 1 Students begin to write simple English structures. They:	Stage 2 Students write in a variety of contexts using simple English structures. They:	Stage 3 Students write English in a variety of contexts with increasing independence and accuracy. They:	Stage 4 Students write English for a variety of purposes using appropriate conventions. They:
– begin to dictate labels, phrases, and sentences to a scribe – print the English alphabet in upper- and lower-case letters – copy written information, following left-to-right and top-to-bottom progression – complete sentence patterns based on familiar and meaningful context and vocabulary – add words to sentence openers to complete a thought – write some personally relevant words – express ideas through drawing, writing in the first language, and labelling – write personal information (e.g., name, address) – participate in shared writing activities in small groups – participate in a variety of prewriting activities – begin to use computers for writing activities	– compose short, simple, patterned sentences based on learned phrases and classroom discussion – write some common and personally relevant words – use capital letters and final punctuation – begin to use basic sentence structures (e.g., statements, questions) – use appropriate formats to write for a variety of purposes (e.g., lists, signs, labels, captions, cards, stories, letters, journals) – use the writing process, with assistance (e.g., participate in structured prewriting activities; make some changes between the initial and final draft) – use computers to begin to develop word-processing skills	– write short compositions, making some use of appropriate verb tenses, prepositions, simple and compound sentences, and descriptions, and beginning to use new vocabulary and idioms – use conventional spelling for most common and personally relevant words – write to record personal experiences and thoughts, to narrate a story, and to convey information – begin to write independently in all subject areas – use the stages of the writing process, with support (e.g., prewriting, producing drafts, and publishing) – write collaboratively with peers	– begin to write competently in all subject areas – contribute to cooperative class writing – use a variety of forms of writing – write short, original compositions using all stages of the writing process – observe most conventions of punctuation

Table A1.5: ESL, Grades 1 to 3 – Orientation

Stage 1 Students begin to adapt to the new environment. They:	Stage 2 Students demonstrate understanding of and adaptation to the new environment. They:	Stage 3 Students demonstrate increasing understanding of and involvement in the new environment. They:	Stage 4 Students demonstrate growing awareness, understanding, and appreciation of their own and others' cultural heritage as part of the Canadian context. They:
– find personally relevant school locations independently – begin to adapt to a variety of teaching strategies used in a Canadian classroom – begin to respond to social situations appropriately – begin to work with a partner on a common academic task – call some classmates and staff by name – communicate critical needs to school staff and peers – develop connections with some staff and peers in the school – follow some classroom and school routines and schedules – rely on the home language and culture to think, communicate, and process new experiences	– ask for assistance and communicate needs – continue to use and take pride in the home language – follow school routines, behaviour expectations, and emergency procedures – interact with peers outside own linguistic or cultural group – participate actively in regular class programs, with modifications – participate in controlled, directed group work (e.g., simple research projects) – participate in most classroom and some school activities (e.g., field trips, sports, clubs) – respond appropriately in most social situations	– continue to use and take pride in the home language – understand and follow school routines, behaviour expectations, and emergency procedures – state basic information about the neighbourhood – actively participate in the daily life of the school – respond appropriately to most teaching approaches (e.g., active learning, the informal classroom atmosphere) – show increasing initiative in cooperative group activities – teach new arrivals key locations in the school	– contribute fully in small, cooperative groups – accept and respect similarities and differences between self and peers – demonstrate pride in own heritage and language – identify and discuss characteristics of the various cultures that make up the community

Table A2.1: ESL, Grades 4 to 6 – Listening

Stage 1 Students understand basic spoken English. They:	Stage 2 Students understand key informatin presented in highly supported contexts in a variety of settings. They:	Stage 3 Students understand social English, but require contextual support to understand academic language. They:	Stage 4 Students understand spoken English in most contexts. They:
– follow simple directions with support from visual cues – respond to short, simple questions – respond briefly to short, simple stories, songs, and poems – respond to familiar conversational topics using single words and short phrases – respond to familiar words, names, phrases, tones of voice, and basic classroom instructions when spoken slowly and clearly	– begin to respond to unseen speakers (e.g., on the telephone) – correctly interpret frequently used verb tenses – participate in social conversations on familiar topics – request clarification when necessary – respond appropriately to body language, tone of voice, pauses, stress, and intonation – understand key vocabulary and concepts related to specific subjects or themes – understand main ideas in visually supported oral presentations containing familiar vocabulary	– respond to unseen speakers (e.g., on the radio, on the telephone) – participate in sustained oral discussions and presentations in small groups – identify main ideas and supporting details in short oral presentations – respond appropriately to formal and informal speech – respond appropriately to vocabulary, statements, questions, and directions in the class – respond to intonation patterns, such as implied commands and tones indicating surprise, emotion, etc. – follow a series of instructions	– identify ideas in oral presentations on a variety of topics, using grade-appropriate vocabulary – respond to spoken English used in social, academic, formal, and informal situations, including some idioms, relevant cultural allusions, and conversational nuances (e.g., teasing, irony, flattery) – take notes from teacher lessons using a supplied written outline as a guide

Table A2.2: ESL, Grades 4 to 6 – Speaking

Stage 1 Students speak English for basic communitcation. They:	**Stage 2** Students speak English with increasing spontaneity and accuracy. They:	**Stage 3** Students initiate conversations and participate in discussions and presentations using a variety of strategies. They:	**Stage 4** Students speak English accurately in most situations. They:
– use short, patterned questions to seek information – share personal information and experiences – express basic needs (e.g., related to washroom, safety) – identify familiar names, objects, and actions – answer specific questions using single words or short phrases – speak with sufficient clarity for teacher comprehension – begin to use (with assistance) subject–predicate order, simple verb tenses, negatives, questions, plurals, pronouns, adjectives, adverbs, common contractions, and basic prepositions of location and direction – imitate some English stress and intonation patterns – use everyday gestures and courtesies to convey meaning – perform simple oral presentations (e.g., rehearsed choral responses, puppet dialogues)	– ask questions – participate in social and academic discussions using short phrases and short sentences – recount familiar events, stories, and key information – rephrase key ideas from written or oral texts, with support – give straightforward directions and instructions – express opinions and emotions – speak with sufficient clarity and accuracy for listener comprehension – speak at almost the pace of first-language speakers, showing some control of stress, timing, and rhythm – use (with some accuracy) prepositions of direction and time and common idioms	– express opinions, basic needs, and requests clearly in most contexts – use conversational strategies such as acknowledgement, reply, agreement, and disagreement – participate in discussions based on classroom themes – make short, effective oral presentations – begin to self-correct grammatical errors – begin to use conditionals and adverb and adjective phrases – use appropriate gestures to convey meaning – use voice to indicate emphasis through pacing, volume, intonation, and stress	– use English appropriately in a range of situations (e.g., to describe, narrate, argue, persuade, summarize, converse) – give accurate, detailed instructions and directions – speak with grade-appropriate vocabulary and sentence structure – speak with fluency and clarity in a large group – express a point of view and explain it in some detail in group discussions – self-correct common grammatical errors – make academic presentations – use idiomatic and colloquial language appropriately

Table A2.3: ESL, Grades 4 to 6 – Reading

Stage 1 Students read and comprehend simple written English. They:	**Stage 2** Students read for specific purposes when background knowledge and vocabulary are familiar. They:	**Stage 3** Students demonstrate increasing independence in a variety of reading tasks, with ongoing support. They:	**Stage 4** Students demonstrate control of grade-appropriate reading tasks. They:
– recognize the English alphabet in both print and script – begin to apply sight-recognition, phonetic, predictive, and contextual reading strategies – recognize frequently used classroom vocabulary – begin to acquire English vocabulary in all subject areas – begin to identify the main ideas of simple passages with familiar vocabulary and supporting visual cues – follow brief written instructions – use learners' and bilingual dictionaries – read simple sentences – use alphabetical order – with assistance, use reading materials for enjoyment and modified school projects	– use reading strategies to assist in determining meaning (e.g., predicting; deducing; inferring; rereading; phonics; recognition of cueing systems, repetition, and word families) – understand short, simple phrases and sentences, instructions, and brief notes in a variety of print media with familiar vocabulary and context – identify main ideas and key information in text – begin to extract information, with assistance, from textbooks, resources, and dictionaries, using headings, margin notes, index, glossary, and graphic organizers – begin to show some fluency in oral reading – choose and read books, with assistance, for a variety of purposes, including personal enjoyment	– skim and scan for key information in reading materials with familiar vocabulary and context – summarize a story, identifying the main idea and some details – read and interpret text at a grade-appropriate level, with some visual support, using context and punctuation clues, phonics, and recognition of familiar vocabulary and word families – choose appropriate materials for research purposes from a variety of sources – read on a regular basis for personal enjoyment – use academic vocabulary, including subject-specific language, with support – use English and bilingual dictionaries – find and use print and media resources, with some support	– analyse unfamiliar text to figure out meaning – identify elements of a story – use vocabulary-acquisition strategies – figure out unfamiliar vocabulary in a familiar context – use skills in independent research to gather information (e.g., from library resources, community resources, print media, and computer resources) – choose and enjoy material for personal reading similar in scope and difficulty to that being read by peers

Table A2.4: ESL, Grades 4 to 6 – Writing

Stage 1 Students begin to write using simple English structures. They:.	**Stage 2** Students write in a variety of contexts using simple English structures. They:	**Stage 3** Students write English in a variety of contexts with increasing independence and accuracy. They:	**Stage 4** Students write English for a variety of purposes using appropriate conventions. They:
– produce the English alphabet in legible cursive and printed form using left-to-right progression and writing on the line – copy written information accurately – begin to apply knowledge of common writing conventions (e.g., punctuation, spelling, capitalization) – begin (with assistance) to use subject–predicate order, simple verb tenses, adjectives, adverbs, and common prepositions of location and direction – write short, coherent, patterned compositions (e.g., short journal entries, lists) on personally relevant topics – begin to use acceptable notebook formats appropriate to subject areas, using titles, dates, charts, and graphs	– begin to make notes, with assistance – begin to use common tenses, spelling, capitalization, and punctuation, with some accuracy – use conventional spelling for common and personally relevant words – write appropriate responses (using short sentences, phrases, or graphic organizers) to written questions based on familiar academic content – begin to use a variety of forms of writing (e.g., short journal entries, notes, dialogues, poems, narratives, reports) – use the writing process, with assistance, producing a final edited copy that is changed from the first draft – use computers to begin to develop word-processing skills	– organize and sequence ideas – write messages, captions, and short notes, with few errors – make notes in some detail on familiar topics – produce prose using appropriate verb tenses, connectors, and subject–verb agreement, with some accuracy – begin to use variety in vocabulary and sentence structure – use paragraphs when writing descriptions and narratives – respond in writing to questions – write short, original compositions on topics of personal or academic interest or knowledge – use the stages of the writing process, with assistance	– use grade-appropriate vocabulary (e.g., spell, understand, and use vocabulary from all subject areas) – produce reports, paragraphs, summaries, and notes on a variety of topics, with few grammatical or spelling errors – use the stages of the writing process – use verb tenses effectively – use word-processing and graphics programs for publishing

Table A2.5: ESL, Grades 4 to 6 – Orientation

Stage 1 Students begin to adapt to the new environment. They:	Stage 2 Students demonstrate understanding of and adaptation to the new environment. They:	Stage 3 Students demonstrate increasing understanding of and involvement in the new environment. They:	Stage 4 Students demonstrate growing awareness, understand-ing, and appreciation of their own and others' cultural heritage as part of the Canadian context. They:
– find personally relevant school locations independently – begin to adapt to a variety of teaching strategies used in a Canadian classroom – begin to respond to social situations appropriately – begin to demonstrate awareness of cultural differences and show pride in self and culture – begin to work with a partner on a common academic task – communicate critical needs to school staff and peers – develop connections with some staff and peers in the school – follow key school routines, behaviour expectations, and emergency procedures – rely on the home language and culture to think, communicate, and process new experiences	– ask for assistance and communicate needs – continue to use and take pride in the home language – follow school routines, behaviour expectations, and procedures – interact with peers outside own linguistic or cultural group – participate actively in regular class program, with modifications – participate in controlled, directed group work – respect cultural differences and show pride in self and own culture – respond with increasing confidence to a variety of teaching strategies (e.g., by expressing own opinions) – use local stores, recreation facilities, and the public library, with adult support – respond appropriately in most social situations	– clearly communicate needs and seek assistance – continue to use and take pride in the home language – explain school routines, behaviour expectations, and procedures to new students, in English or a shared first language – state basic information about the neighbourhood, municipality, province, and Canada – participate in all regular class activities – participate in some school and community activities – respond appropriately to most teaching approaches – show increasing initiative in group activities – show sensitivity to and appreciation of diverse languages and cultures	– contribute fully in small, cooperative groups – understand and respect different cultural values – show pride in and knowledge of own culture and language – express interest in the cultures and languages of peers – discuss the significance of some local current events – learn effectively from a variety o f teaching approaches (e.g., question and answer, cooperative/independent research) – participate in a variety of school and community activities

Table A3.1: ESL, Grades 7 and 8 – Listening

Stage 1 Students understand basic spoken English. They:	Stage 2 Students understand key information presented in highly supported contexts in a variety of settings. They:	Stage 3 Students understand social English, but require contextual support to understand academic language. They:	Stage 4 Students understand spoken English in most contexts. They:
– follow simple directions with support from visual cues – respond to short, simple questions – respond briefly to short, simple stories, songs, and poems – respond to familiar conversational topics using single words and short phrases – respond to gestures, courtesies, tones of voice, and basic classroom instructions	– participate in conversations on familiar topics – respond to vocabulary, questions, and instructions in a familiar context – request clarification when necessary – respond appropriately to body language, tone of voice, pauses, stress, and intonation – understand key vocabulary and concepts related to specific subjects or themes – understand main ideas in visually supported oral presentations containing familiar vocabulary	– participate in sustained oral discussions and presentations in small groups – identify main ideas and supporting details in short oral presentations – respond appropriately to formal and informal speech – respond to new vocabulary, statements, questions, and directions in class – respond to intonation patterns in speech – respond to unseen speakers (e.g., on the radio, on the telephone) – follow a series of instructions – take notes from teacher lessons presented orally, using a supplied written outline as a guide – identify key ideas in a variety of media works	– identify ideas in a variety of oral presentations, on a range of topics, using grade-appropriate vocabulary – respond to complex sentence structures in discussions – respond to spoken English used in social, academic, formal, and informal situations, including some idioms, relevant cultural allusions, and conversational nuances (e.g., teasing, irony, flattery, humour, sarcasm) – take notes from teacher lessons using a supplied written outline as a guide

Table A3.2: ESL, Grades 7 and 8 – Speaking

Stage 1 Students speak English for basic communication. They:	Stage 2 Students speak English with increasing spontaneity and accuracy. They:	Stage 3 Students initiate conversations and participate in discussions and presentations using a variety of strategies. They:	Stage 4 Students speak English accurately in most situations. They:
– use short, patterned questions to seek information – share personal information and experiences – express basic needs (e.g., related to washroom, safety) – identify familiar names, objects, and actions – answer specific questions using single words or short phrases – speak with sufficient clarity for teacher comprehension – begin to use (with assistance) subject–predicate order, simple verb tenses, negatives, questions, plurals, pronouns, adjectives, adverbs, common contractions, and basic prepositions of location and direction – imitate some English stress and intonation patterns – use everyday gestures and courtesies to convey meaning – perform simple oral presentations, (e.g., role plays, dialogues)	– ask questions – participate in social and academic discussions using short phrases and short sentences – recount familiar events, stories, and key information – give straightforward directions and instructions – express opinions, emotions, wishes, and needs – speak with sufficient clarity and accuracy for listener comprehension – speak at almost the pace of first-language speakers, showing some control of stress, timing, and rhythm – use (with some accuracy) common tenses, adjectives, adverbs, conjunctions, prepositions of direction and time, and common idioms	– use conversational strategies such as acknowledgement, inquiry, reply, agreement, and disagreement – participate in discussions based on classroom themes – give instructions and directions with some detail – make short, effective oral presentations – speak clearly enough to be easily understood by peers and teachers – begin to self-correct grammatical errors – begin to use implication, figurative language, passive voice, conditionals, and adjective and adverb phrases – use gestures and voice to indicate emphasis through pacing, volume, intonation, and stress	– use English appropriately in a range of situations (e.g., to describe, narrate, argue, persuade, summarize, converse) – give accurate, detailed instructions and directions – speak with grade-appropriate vocabulary and sentence structure – speak with fluency and clarity in a large group – express a point of view and explain it in some detail in group discussions – self-correct common grammatical errors – make academic presentations using resources – use idiomatic and colloquial language appropriately

Table A3.3: ESL, Grades 7 and 8 – Reading

Stage 1 Students read and comprehend simple written English. They:	**Stage 2** Students read for specific purposes when background knowledge and vocabulary are familiar. They:	**Stage 3** Students demonstrate increasing independence in a variety of reading tasks, with ongoing support. They:	**Stage 4** Students demonstrate control of grade-appropriate reading tasks. They:
– recognize the alphabet in both print and script – apply sight recognition, phonetic, predictive, and contextual reading strategies – recognize frequently used classroom vocabulary – begin to acquire English vocabulary in all subject areas – identify the main ideas of simple passages with familiar vocabulary and supporting visual cues – follow brief written instructions – use learners' and bilingual dictionaries – use alphabetical order – use reading materials for enjoyment and modified school projects, with assistance	– use reading strategies to assist in deriving meaning (e.g., predicting; deducing; inferring; rereading; phonics; recognition of cueing systems, repetition, and word families) – begin to use vocabulary-acquisition strategies (e.g., recognize changes caused by addition of prefixes and suffixes; hypothesize meaning of unfamiliar vocabulary in a familiar context; use an English dictionary and thesaurus) – understand short, simple phrases and sentences, instructions, and brief notes in material with familiar vocabulary and context – identify main ideas and key information in text – extract information from textbooks, resources, and dictionaries, using headings, margin notes, index, glossary, graphic organizers, et cetera – begin to show some fluency in oral reading – choose and read books for a variety of purposes, including personal enjoyment	– skim and scan for key information in reading materials with familiar vocabulary and context – predict, summarize, and make judgements about class texts – use some vocabulary-acquisition strategies – read and interpret visually supported text at a grade-appropriate level – use academic vocabulary, including subject-specific language, with support – use English and bilingual dictionaries – show developing fluency in oral reading – locate and evaluate library materials for research purposes, with support	– analyse unfamiliar text to figure out its meaning – use vocabulary-acquisition strategies – understand and respond to extended text selections – use the various parts of a textbook to find information (e.g., glossary, margin notes, table of contents, index) – use skills in independent research to gather information (e.g., in the library, in the community) – choose and enjoy material for personal reading similar in scope and difficulty to that being read by peers – identify elements of a story

Table A3.4: ESL, Grades 7 and 8 – Writing

Stage 1 Students begin to write simple English structures. They:	**Stage 2** Students write in a variety of contexts using simple English structures. They:	**Stage 3** Students write English in a variety of contexts with increasing independence and accuracy. They:	**Stage 4** Students write English for a variety of purposes using appropriate conventions. They:
– produce the English alphabet in legible cursive and printed form using left-to-right progression and writing on the line – copy blackboard notes and text accurately – begin to apply knowledge of basic writing conventions (e.g., punctuation, spelling, capitalization) – begin to use simple verb tenses, questions, plurals, and common prepositions of location, direction, and time – write short, coherent, patterned compositions (e.g., short journal entries, lists) on personally relevant topics – begin to use acceptable notebook formats appropriate to subject areas, using titles, dates, charts, and graphs	– begin to make notes, with assistance – begin to use common tenses, spelling, capitalization, and punctuation, with some accuracy – use conventional spelling for common and personally relevant words – write appropriate responses (using short sentences, phrases, or graphic organizers) to written questions based on familiar academic content – begin to use a variety of forms of writing (e.g., short journal entries, notes, dialogues, poems, narratives, reports) – use the writing process, with assistance, producing a final edited copy that is changed from the first draft – use computers to begin to develop word-processing skills	– organize and sequence ideas effectively – make notes in some detail on familiar topics – produce prose using appropriate verb tenses, connectors, subject–verb agreement, noun, adjective, and adverb phrases and clauses, and conventional spelling, with some accuracy – begin to use variety in vocabulary and sentence structure – use paragraphs when writing descriptions and narratives – respond in writing to questions on personal and academic topics – write short, original compositions, summaries, and reports on topics of personal and academic interest or knowledge – write letters, following the appropriate conventions – use the stages of the writing process, with assistance	– use grade-appropriate vocabulary (e.g., demonstrate knowledge of derivations and word families; formulate definitions; spell, understand, and use vocabulary from all subject areas) – produce reports, editorials, paragraphs, summaries, and notes on a variety of topics, with few grammatical or spelling errors – use the stages of the writing process (e.g., prewriting activities, revising, editing, conferencing, and publishing)

Table A3.5: ESL, Grades 7 and 8 – Orientation

Stage 1 Students begin to adapt to the new environment. They:	Stage 2 Students demonstrate understanding of and adaptation to the new environment. They:	Stage 3 Students demonstrate increasing understanding of and involvement in the new environment. They:	Stage 4 Students demonstrate growing awareness, understanding, and appreciation of their own and others' cultural heritage as part of the Canadian context. They:
– find personally relevant school locations independently – begin to adapt to a variety of teaching strategies used in a Canadian classroom – begin to respond to social situations appropriately – demonstrate awareness of cultural differences and show pride in self and culture – begin to use community resources, such as banks and stores – begin to work with a partner on a common academic task – communicate critical needs to school staff and peers – understand and follow essential school schedules, behaviour expectations, routines, and emergency procedures – rely on the home language and culture to think, communicate, and process new experiences	– ask for assistance and communicate needs – begin to participate in school activities, clubs, and teams – continue to use, take pride in, and respect the home language – state basic information about the neighbourhood, municipality, province, and Canada – interact with peers outside own linguistic or cultural group – participate in controlled, directed group work – respect cultural differences and take pride in own culture – respond with increasing confidence to a variety of teaching strategies	– clearly communicate needs and seek assistance in the school and in the community – continue to use and take pride in the home language – explain school norms, routines, behaviour expectations, and emergency procedures to new students, in English or a shared first language – participate in class, school, and community activities – respond appropriately to most teaching approaches – show increasing initiative in group activities – show sensitivity to and appreciation of diverse languages and cultures	– contribute fully in cooperative groups – understand and respect different cultural values – show pride in and knowledge of own culture and language – recognize the benefits and responsibilities of living in a diverse society – discuss the significance of some current events at the local, national, and international levels – learn effectively from a variety of teaching approaches – use resources in the school and the surrounding community

B. Stages of Second-Language Acquisition and Literacy Development for ELD Students

Table B1.1: ELD, Grades 1 to 3 – Oral Expression and Language Knowledge

Stage 1 Students begin to use standard Canadian English in appropriate contexts. They:	Stage 2 Students demonstrate increasing use of standard Canadian English in appropriate contexts. They:	Stage 3 Students demonstrate independence in using standard Canadian English in appropriate contexts. They:
– request clarification or confirmation when necessary – describe personal experiences – retell simple stories – participate in chants and/or choral speaking	– participate in classroom and group discussions – share personal experiences and opinions – retell stories with some detail – present puppet plays – use different varieties of spoken English (e.g., standard Canadian English, regional languages, interlanguages) in appropriate contexts	– contribute to classroom and group discussions – discuss and interpret stories, movies, and news events – participate in role-playing activities

Table B1.2: ELD, Grades 1 to 3 – Reading

Stage 1 Students read and comprehend simple written English. They:	Stage 2 Students read for specific purposes when background knowledge and vocabulary are familiar. They:	Stage 3 Students demonstrate increasing independence in a variety of reading tasks, with support as needed. They:	Stage 4 Students demonstrate control of grade-appropriate reading tasks. They:
– understand concepts of print (e.g., progression from left to right, top to bottom) – recognize the alphabet in print – use alphabetical order – read pictures and use picture clues – recognize frequently used words (e.g., the, went, in) – begin to use phonics, context clues, and sight recognition for comprehension in pattern books, chart stories, songs, chants, and rhymes – select and read, with assistance, print material appropriate to their reading ability, interests, and age – begin to use primary dictionaries	– recognize the alphabet in script – scan for details such as letter sounds or specific words – select main ideas in short, familiar passages – begin to use reading strategies to derive meaning from text (e.g., predicting, deducing, rereading, phonics, recognizing word families) – begin to show fluency in oral reading, using some correct phrasing and rhythm – use the school library, with assistance, to select reading material for personal enjoyment and information – use primary dictionaries	– understand grade-appropriate text, with assistance – select main ideas in short passages from a variety of sources – extend their academic/technical vocabulary in curriculum subject areas – choose a variety of personal reading materials – begin to use grade-appropriate resources such as graphic organizers, class word lists, theme-book collections, environmental print, and tables of contents	– understand grade-appropriate text that may be unfamiliar and unsupported by visual context clues, and that may contain complex sentence structures – use research skills in the classroom and school library – begin to choose personal reading material

Table B1.3: ELD, Grades 1 to 3 – Writing

Stage 1 Students begin to write using basic structures. They:	Stage 2 Students write for a variety of purposes, with support. They:	Stage 3 Students write in a variety of contexts with increasing independence and accuracy. They:	Stage 4 Students write for a variety of purposes, applying knowledge of the conventions of written English appropriately. They:
– print the alphabet in upper- and lower-case letters – copy words, phrases, and sentences – write personal information (e.g., name, address) – write about personal experiences or classroom discussion, using patterned sentences – participate in a variety of prewriting activities such as dramatic play, drawing, and talk – spell some personally relevant words – begin to use computers for word processing	– write invitations, thank-you notes, and personal stories – write short paragraphs based on classroom discussion – use the writing process (e.g., participate in structured prewriting activities; make some changes between the initial and the final draft) – spell most common and personally relevant words – use computers for word processing	– write about personal experiences, thoughts, feelings, stories, and information with some fluency – use a range of vocabulary and sentence structures – demonstrate an awareness that the writing process involves prewriting, drafting, and publishing – apply knowledge of the conventions of standard Canadian English in their writing, with increasing accuracy (e.g., use capital letters and periods; use conventional spelling for common and personally relevant words) – begin to write independently in all subject areas	– use a variety of writing formats – write short, original compositions using all steps of the writing process, including publication – use correct punctuation and spelling most of the time – write with some competence in all subject areas, with a clear focus, coherent organization, and varied vocabulary

Table B1.4: ESL, Grades 1 to 3 – Orientation

Stage 1 Students begin to adapt to new environments, both personal and academic. They:	Stage 2 Students demonstrate understanding of and adaptation to new environments, both personal and academic. They:	Stage 3 Students demonstrate increasing understanding of and involvement in new environments, both personal and academic. They:	Stage 4 Students demonstrate awareness of self and others as part of the Canadian context. They:
– take pride in and respect their own culture – locate key school locations (e.g., washrooms) – begin to understand and follow essential school norms, schedules, routines, and emergency procedures – ask for assistance and communicate needs to appropriate school personnel and/or peers – begin to relate information about Canada (e.g., climate, holidays, safety) to their own activities and interests – work with a partner on a common academic task – begin to adapt to a variety of teaching approaches and strategies used in a Canadian classroom	– respect other cultures – participate with increasing comfort and confidence in classroom activities – demonstrate understanding of basic information about the community and about Canada – participate in directed group work such as simple research projects – respond with increasing confidence to a variety of teaching approaches and strategies (e.g., an informal classroom atmosphere, active learning, the use of games as a learning activity, activities that involve asking questions of a teacher)	– show interest in other cultures – explain school norms, routines, behaviour expectations, and emergency procedures to new students – discuss some current events – show increasing initiative in cooperative group activities such as research projects – respond appropriately to most teaching approaches and strategies (e.g., an informal classroom atmosphere, active learning, use of games as a learning activity, activities that involve asking questions of a teacher)	– identify and appreciate the contributions of various cultures within Canada – contribute fully in a small, cooperative group to create a final product or presentation – learn effectively from a variety of teaching approaches and strategies (e.g., an informal classroom atmosphere, active learning, the use of games as a learning activity, activities that involve asking questions of a teacher)

Table B2.1: ELD, Grades 4 to 6 – Oral Expression and Language Knowledge

Stage 1 Students begin to use standard Canadian English in appropriate contexts. They:	Stage 2 Students demonstrate increasing use of standard Canadian English in appropriate contexts. They:	Stage 3 Students demonstrate independence in using standard Canadian English in appropriate contexts. They:
– respond to oral instruction and information in standard Canadian English in school settings – request clarification or confirmation, when necessary, about assembly routines, library procedures, and announcements – share personal information and experiences – retell simple stories – present a prepared story or poem – participate in choral speaking – begin to recognize different varieties of spoken English (e.g., standard Canadian English, interlanguages, regional languages) and their appropriateness for different contexts and purposes	– participate in classroom and group discussion – begin to use language to explain, persuade, and negotiate (e.g., to make requests and settle arguments) – share personal experiences and opinions – retell stories with details – present book talks and projects – participate in role-playing activities – begin to monitor their own pronunciation and grammar when speaking – recognize different varieties of spoken English (e.g., standard Canadian English, interlanguages, regional languages) and begin to use them appropriately in specific situations (e.g., social conversations, classroom talk, presentations)	– participate in classroom discussions and presentations using a variety of techniques such as explaining, describing, and summarizing – use language to explain, persuade, negotiate, and clarify – select vocabulary appropriate to specific needs and situations – compare, interpret, and evaluate stories, movies, and articles – present skits and short dramas – monitor their own pronunciation and grammar when speaking – use varieties of spoken English (e.g., standard Canadian English, interlanguages, regional languages) appropriately in specific situations (e.g., social conversations, introductions, explanations)

Table B2.2: ELD, Grades 4 to 6 – Reading

Stage 1 Students read and comprehend simple written English. They:	Stage 2 Students read for specific purposes when background knowledge and vocabulary are familiar. They:	Stage 3 Students demonstrate increasing independence in a variety of reading tasks, with support as needed. They:	Stage 4 Students demonstrate control of grade-appropriate reading tasks. They:
– understand concepts of print (e.g., progression from left to right, top to bottom) – recognize the alphabet in both print and script – use alphabetical order – recognize vocabulary common to their environment (e.g., the school, the community) – recognize frequently used words found in most texts – begin to recognize subject-specific vocabulary – use learners' and visual dictionaries – recognize the main ideas of simple passages – begin to develop the habit of daily reading for enjoyment and information	– understand passages in text with familiar vocabulary and context – begin to use reading strategies to derive meaning from text (e.g., recognizing word families, cueing systems, and repetition of words or phrases; predicting; deducing; inferring; rereading; phonics) – expand academic vocabulary (i.e., of subject-related words and expressions) – begin to locate information in textbooks and resources by using tables of contents, headings, margin notes, index, glossary, photographs, and graphic organizers – recognize main ideas and key information in text with familiar background and vocabulary from a variety of genres – begin to read aloud, with fluency and appropriate phrasing and rhythm – choose and read books, with assistance, for a variety of purposes, including personal enjoyment	– understand grade-appropriate text with assistance – skim and scan text for key information – begin to use vocabulary-acquisition strategies (e.g., recognizing how adding a prefix or suffix changes the meaning of a word; hypothesizing about the meaning of unfamiliar words; using a dictionary to check meaning and usage and identify parts of speech) – use dictionary skills with increasing independence – begin to compare main ideas and key information from a variety of sources – read on a regular basis, with considerable understanding	– understand unfamiliar text that may contain complex sentence structures and have few visual context clues – use vocabulary-acquisition strategies – use research skills to gather information from library resources, community resources, print media, computers, and CD-ROMs – analyse and evaluate ideas and information – choose a variety of personal reading materials

Table B2.3: ELD, Grades 4 to 6 – Writing

Stage 1 Students begin to write using basic structures. They:	**Stage 2** Students write for a variety of purposes, with support. They:	**Stage 3** Students write in a variety of contexts with increasing independence and accuracy. They:	**Stage 4** Students write for a variety of purposes, applying knowledge of the conventions of written English appropriately. They:
– print and write the alphabet in upper- and lower-case letters – copy words, phrases, and sentences – write short, patterned compositions (e.g., personal information, dialogues) – write short journal entries, narratives, lists, stories, and poems, with assistance – begin to keep notebooks appropriate to subject areas – begin to apply the conventions of standard Canadian English in their writing (e.g., correct punctuation, spelling, and capitalization; appropriate tenses) – begin to use computers for word processing	– use cursive writing – begin to use, in guided situations, a variety of forms, such as short journal entries, notes, narratives, and reports, to answer questions, convey facts and information, express personal views, and describe scenes, events, and people – organize information around a central idea using graphic organizers (e.g., charts, webs, graphs, diagrams, tables) – begin to make notes (e.g., on texts, videos) – use the writing process, with assistance (e.g., participate in prewriting activities, write drafts, revise content independently or with a peer, produce an edited copy of written work) – apply knowledge of the conventions of standard Canadian English in their writing, with increasing accuracy – use computers for word processing	– write in a variety of forms on topics of personal and academic interest – make notes in some detail on familiar topics – use the stages of the writing process, with assistance, to produce an edited copy of written work – produce, with some consistency, appropriately structured prose with suitable verb tenses and connectors, subject–verb agreement, noun, adjective, and adverb phrases and clauses, and correct spelling – use a varied vocabulary and a range of sentence structures – use computers for a variety of writing tasks	– produce paragraphs, summaries, and notes on a variety of topics, with few grammatical or spelling errors – use the writing process – spell, understand, and use vocabulary from all subject areas – write with some competence in all subject areas, with a clear focus, coherent organization, and varied vocabulary

Table B2.4: ELD, Grades 4 to 6 – Orientation

Stage 1 Students begin to adapt to new environments, both personal and academic. They:	**Stage 2** Students demonstrate understanding of and adaptation to new environments, both personal and academic. They:	**Stage 3** Students demonstrate increasing understanding of and involvement in new environments, both personal and academic. They:	**Stage 4** Students demonstrate awareness of self and others as part of the Canadian context. They:
– take pride in and respect their own culture – begin to understand and follow essential school norms, schedules, and emergency procedures, and accept the importance of regular school attendance and punctuality – begin to understand teacher expectations and follow classroom routines (e.g., doing homework, coming to class prepared) – ask for assistance and communicate needs to appropriate school personnel and/or peers – identify specific times and locations in which to do school work and/or study – begin to relate information about Canadian culture, climate, holidays, and geography to their own activities and interests – work with a partner on a shared academic task – begin to adapt to a variety of teaching approaches and strategies used in a Canadian classroom	– respect other cultures – locate and use school services (e.g., guidance counsellor, library) – participate with increasing ease and confidence in classroom activities – use some community facilities and resources (e.g., the library) – begin to accept responsibility for own learning by recognizing consequences and managing own time – demonstrate understanding of basic information about the neighbourhood, municipality, province, and Canada – participate in directed group work – respond with increasing confidence to a variety of teaching approaches and strategies – begin to identify personal and educational goals	– show interest in other cultures – explain school norms, routines, behaviour expectations, and emergency procedures to new students – use school and some community resources appropriately (e.g., public library, recreation centre) – accept responsibility for own learning by making up missed work, recognizing consequences, and managing own time – discuss current events – show increasing initiative in group activities – respond appropriately to most teaching approaches and strategies – locate and use information, with assistance, in order to pursue personal, educational, and career goals and opportunities	– identify and appreciate the contributions of various cultures – explain the significance of current events at the local, national, and international levels – contribute fully in a small, cooperative group to create a final product or presentation – learn effectively from a variety of teaching approaches and strategies – locate and use information in order to pursue personal, educational, and career goals

Table B3.1: ELD, Grades 7 and 8 – Oral Expression and Language Knowledge

Stage 1 Students begin to use standard Canadian English in appropriate contexts. They:	Stage 2 Students demonstrate increasing use of standard Canadian English in appropriate contexts. They:	Stage 3 Students demonstrate independence in using standard Canadian English in appropriate contexts. They:
– respond to oral instructions and information in standard Canadian English in school settings – request clarification or confirmation, when necessary, about assembly routines, library procedures, how to get a public transit pass, and announcements – share personal information and experiences – retell stories – present a prepared story or poem – participate in choral speaking – begin to recognize different varieties of spoken English (e.g., standard Canadian English, interlanguages, regional languages) and their appropriateness for specific contexts and purposes (e.g., social conversations, classroom talk)	– participate in classroom and group discussions – begin to use language to explain, persuade, and negotiate (e.g., to make requests and settle arguments) – share personal experiences and opinions – retell stories with details – present book talks and projects – participate in role-playing activities – begin to monitor their own pronunciation and grammar when speaking – recognize different varieties of spoken English (e.g., standard Canadian English, interlanguages, regional languages) and begin to use them appropriately in specific situations (e.g., social conversations, classroom talk)	– participate in discussions and presentations using a variety of techniques such as explaining, describing, and summarizing – use language to explain, persuade, negotiate, and clarify – select vocabulary appropriate to specific needs and situations – compare, interpret, and evaluate stories, movies, and articles – make a presentation to the class – present skits and short dramas – monitor their own pronunciation and grammar when speaking – use varieties of spoken English (e.g., standard Canadian English, interlanguages, regional languages) appropriately – recognize that languages evolve over time in response to historical, sociological, and economic pressures

Table B3.2: ELD, Grades 7 to 8 – Reading

Stage 1 Students read and comprehend simple written English. They:	Stage 2 Students read for specific purposes when background knowledge and vocabulary are familiar. They:	Stage 3 Students demonstrate increasing independence in a variety of reading tasks, with support as needed. They:	Stage 4 Students demonstrate control of grade-appropriate reading tasks. They:
– recognize the alphabet in both print and script and use alphabetical order – recognize vocabulary common to their environment (e.g., the school, the community) – recognize frequently used words found in most texts – begin to apply some reading strategies (e.g., sight recognition, phonics, using context clues) to derive meaning from text – begin to recognize subject-specific vocabulary – use learners' and visual dictionaries – recognize the main ideas of simple passages – begin to read familiar passages aloud with some fluency – begin to develop the habit of daily reading for enjoyment and information	– understand short phrases and sentences, instructions, and brief notes in a variety of print media with familiar vocabulary and context – begin to use reading strategies to derive meaning from texts (e.g., recognizing cueing systems and word families; predicting; deducing; inferring; rereading; phonics) – expand academic vocabulary (i.e., of subject-related words and expressions) – begin to locate information in textbooks and resources by using tables of contents, headings, margin notes, index, glossary, photographs, and graphic organizers – recognize main ideas and key information in text with familiar background and vocabulary from a variety of genres – begin to read aloud, with fluency and appropriate phrasing and rhythm, passages with familiar vocabulary and background – choose and read books, with assistance or independently, for a variety of purposes, including personal enjoyment	– understand grade-appropriate text, with assistance – skim and scan text for key information – begin to use vocabulary-acquisition strategies (e.g., recognizing how adding a prefix or suffix changes the meaning of a word; hypothesizing about the meaning of unfamiliar words in a familiar context; using a dictionary to check meaning and usage and identify parts of speech) – use dictionary skills with increasing independence – compare main ideas and key information from a variety of sources – read on a regular basis with considerable understanding	– understand unfamiliar text that may contain complex sentence structures and have few visual context clues – use a range of vocabulary-acquisition strategies – independently use research skills to gather information from library resources, community resources, print media, and CD-ROMs – analyse and evaluate ideas and information – choose a variety of personal reading materials

Table B3.3: ELD, Grades 7 and 8 – Writing

Stage 1 Students begin to write using basic structures. They:	Stage 2 Students write for a variety of purposes, with support. They:	Stage 3 Students write in a variety of contexts with increasing independence and accuracy. They:	Stage 4 Students write for a variety of purposes, applying knowledge of the conventions of written English appropriately. They:
– print and write the alphabet in upper- and lower-case letters – copy words, phrases, and sentences – write short, patterned compositions (e.g., personal information, dialogues) – write short journal entries, narratives, lists, stories, and poems, with assistance – begin to keep notebooks appropriate to subject areas – begin to apply the conventions of standard Canadian English in their writing (e.g., correct punctuation, spelling, and capitalization; plural markers; subject–verb agreement; appropriate tenses) – begin to use computers for word processing	– begin to use, in guided situations, a variety of forms, such as short journal entries, notes, dialogues, narratives, and reports, to answer questions, convey facts and information, express personal views and opinions, and describe scenes, events, and people – organize information around a central idea using graphic organizers (e.g., charts, webs, graphs, diagrams, tables) – begin to make notes (e.g., on texts, videos) – use the writing process, with assistance, to produce an edited copy of written work – apply knowledge of the conventions of standard Canadian English in their writing, with increasing accuracy – use computers for word processing	– write in a variety of forms on topics of personal and academic interest – make notes in some detail on familiar topics – use the writing process, with assistance, to produce an edited copy of written work – produce, with some consistency, appropriately structured prose with suitable verb tenses and connectors, subject–verb agreement, noun, adjective, and adverb phrases and clauses, and correct spelling – use a varied vocabulary and a range of sentence structures – use computers for a variety of writing tasks	– produce stories, reports, summaries, and notes on a variety of topics, with few grammatical or spelling errors – use the writing process – spell, understand, and use vocabulary from all subject areas – write with some competence in all subject areas, with a clear focus, coherent organization, and varied vocabulary

Table B3.4: ELD, Grades 7 and 8 – Orientation

Stage 1 Students begin to adapt to the new environment, both personal and academic. They:	Stage 2 Students demonstrate understanding of and adaptation to new environments, both personal and academic. They:	Stage 3 Students demonstrate increasing understanding of and involvement in new environments, both personal and academic. They:	Stage 4 Students demonstrate awareness of self and others as part of the Canadian context. They:
– take pride in and respect their own culture – begin to understand and follow essential school norms, schedules, and emergency procedures and to accept the importance of regular school attendance and punctuality – begin to understand teacher expectations and follow classroom routines (e.g., doing homework, coming to class prepared) – communicate needs to appropriate school personnel and/or peers and ask them for assistance – identify specific times and locations in which to do school work and/or study – begin to relate information about Canadian culture, climate, holidays, and geography to their own activities and interests – work with a partner on a shared academic task – begin to adapt to a variety of teaching approaches and strategies used in a Canadian classroom	– respect other cultures – locate and use school services (e.g., guidance counsellor, library) – participate with increasing comfort and confidence in classroom activities – use some community resources (e.g., the library, a bank) – begin to accept responsibility for own learning by recognizing consequences and managing own time – demonstrate understanding of basic information about the neighbourhood, municipality, province, and Canada – participate in directed group work – respond with increasing confidence to a variety of teaching approaches and strategies – begin to identify personal and educational goals	– show interest in other cultures – explain school norms, routines, behaviour expectations, and emergency procedures to new students – accept responsibility for own learning and begin to use effective study skills (e.g., summarizing, memorizing, rehearsing) – use school and community resources and facilities appropriately – explain the significance of some current events at the local, national, and international levels – show increasing initiative in group activities – respond appropriately to most teaching approaches and strategies – locate and use information, with assistance, in order to pursue personal, educational, and career goals and opportunities	– identify and appreciate the contributions of various cultures – recognize the benefits and responsibilities of living in a diverse society – identify and use effective study skills – explain elements of the Canadian political system – contribute fully in a small group – learn effectively from a variety of teaching approaches and strategies – locate and use information in order to pursue personal, educational, and career goals